THE LEAGUE OF NATIONS.

BY THE

RT. HON. SIR FREDERICK POLLOCK, BT.,

BARRISTER-AT-LAW, D.C.L., LL.D.

*Correspondent of the Institute of France ; Associate Member of the
Royal Academy of Belgium.*

Fiat iustitia ne pereat mundus.
Leibnitz

" We fought to gain a lasting peace, and it is our supreme duty to take
every measure to secure it. For that nothing is more essential than a strong
and enduring League of Nations."—*The King's message to the League of
Nations Union, October 13th, 1919.*

THE LAWBOOK EXCHANGE, LTD.
Clark, New Jersey

ISBN 978-1-58477-247-7

Lawbook Exchange edition 2003, 2020

The quality of this reprint is equivalent to the quality of the original work.

THE LAWBOOK EXCHANGE, LTD.
33 Terminal Avenue
Clark, New Jersey 07066-1321

*Please see our website for a selection of our other publications
and fine facsimile reprints of classic works of legal history:*
www.lawbookexchange.com

Library of Congress Cataloging-in-Publication Data

Pollock, Frederick, Sir, 1845-1937.
   The League of Nations / by the Rt. Hon. Sir Frederick Pollock.
     p. cm.
   Originally published: London: Stevens and Sons, 1920.
   "[P]ractical exposition of the Covenant of the League of Nations"
--Preface.
   Includes bibliographical references and index.
   ISBN 1-58477-247-6 (cloth : alk. paper)
    1. League of Nations. Covenant. I. Title.

JZ4872 .P65 2002
  341.22—dc2l   2002025943

Printed in the United States of America on acid-free paper

THE LEAGUE OF NATIONS.

BY THE

RT. HON. SIR FREDERICK POLLOCK, BT.,

BARRISTER-AT-LAW, D.C.L., LL.D.

Correspondent of the Institute of France; Associate Member of the Royal Academy of Belgium.

Fiat iustitia ne pereat mundus.

Leibnitz

" We fought to gain a lasting peace, and it is our supreme duty to take every measure to secure it. For that nothing is more essential than a strong and enduring League of Nations."—*The King's message to the League of Nations Union, October* 13th, 1919.

LONDON:

STEVENS AND SONS, LIMITED,

119 & 120, CHANCERY LANE,

Law Publishers.

1920.

ROBERTO CECIL

INTER VIROS VERE PACIFICOS INSIGNI.

PREFACE.

THE purpose of this book is to give a practical
exposition of the Covenant of the League of
Nations, with so much introduction as appears
proper for enabling the reader to understand the
conditions under which the League was formed
and has to commence its work. If here and
there I have been tempted to wander from the
strait way, the digressions are not long enough
to call for any special apology.

No systematic attempt has yet been made to
deal with the bibliography of the subject, which
is indeed growing so fast that such an attempt
would be premature. I have therefore not
thought it useful to print a general list of
authorities which would be imperfect at best. At
the heads of chapters, however, especially the
introductory ones, I have given references to
authentic documents and to other publications
which seemed fitted to assist the reader in verify-
ing the facts or undertaking fuller research.
These references make no pretence to complete-
ness and imply no judgment of any kind on
works not cited; among those I have not seen or
not used there may be many quite as good as
those I have myself found profitable. I trust

however that the selection, such as it is, may be helpful.

For like reasons I do not profess to appraise the individual merit of the statesmen and authors whose labours prepared the way for the establishment of the League. A justly proportioned view is hardly possible in our time.

Some general acquaintance with the notorious events of recent years is assumed; I see no middle course between taking so much for granted and writing a history of the war. For my part I have no higher ambition than that, when the time is ripe for a definitive record, this volume may save the future historian some trouble.

F. P.

Lincoln's Inn,
     November 30th, 1919.

Note.—In the course of November, 1919, the Senate of the United States refused to ratify the Peace Treaty with Germany save with various reservations to the Covenant. Those reservations were drawn without due consideration, being for the most part amplified statements of what is expressed or clearly implied in the text of the Covenant itself. The result was a deadlock involving at best regrettable delay, but down to the end of November the issue seemed likely to be a compromise of some kind compatible with the adhesion of the United States to the League. It must be plainly understood, however, that there can be no true League unless the members are pledged in principle to mutual defence and support against external aggression. "Covenants without the sword are but words, and of no strength to secure a man at all." It will be a long time before we can afford to forget that saying of Thomas Hobbes.

(ix)

CONTENTS.

—◆—

BOOK I.—Introductory.

—◆—

CHAPTER I.

THE OLDER EUROPEAN ORDER.

PAGE

War, peace and government 1
Arbitration in the Middle Ages 3
Early federal alliances 4
Plans of general confederation 5
Early international law: Balance of Power 8
The system of the Congress of Vienna 10
The Crimean war and after 11
Later European Congresses 13
Dissolution of the Concert in 1908 15
Summary of stages in the political system before 1914 ... 15
    Note A.—Treaty between Henry II. of England
    and Philip II. of France 16

CHAPTER II.

METHODS OF INTERNATIONAL ARBITRATION.

Ancient practice revived in modern times 17
Standing treaties 18
Arbitration distinguished from mediation 19
Its judicial character 20
Imperfection of transitory jurisdiction 22

CHAPTER II.—*continued*.

	PAGE
Neither awards nor judicial decisions infallible	24
Pretended necessity of war	25
Law and reason in international arbitration	28
Rules not wanting as alleged	30
Compromise in decisions	31
Free choice of arbitrators	32
The *Alabama* case	33
Its effect in reviving arbitration	34
Composition of arbitral tribunals	34
Form of arbitration treaties	36
Treaties of unlimited reference to Peace Commissions...	39
Note B.—Conventions made by Great Britain with France and the U.S.	40
Note C.—Peace Commission treaty between Great Britain and the U.S.	43

CHAPTER III.

THE HAGUE TRIBUNAL.

The Peace Conference of 1899	48
of 1907	49
The Convention as to settlement of disputes	50
Special commissions and reports: the Dogger Bank case	51
The danger averted	53
Provisions for arbitration	53
Procedure	56
Summary procedure	58
Is the Tribunal a court of justice?	58
Project of a permanent judicial court	60
The German attitude	64
Renewal of the scheme in 1914..............................	64

CHAPTER IV.

THE LEAGUE IN SIGHT.

PAGE

Methods of settling disputes down to 1914 66

Expectations of improvement 67

Federalist theories 69

Foundation of the American League to enforce Peace... 70

Militarist and pacifist extreme views 72

British and Continental societies 73

Allied societies in conference 74

Agreement of the Western Allies in the principle 74

Lord Parker of Waddington's last speech 75

Question as to manner and time of constituting the
    League 77

Gen. Smuts's pamphlet 77

American unofficial draft 79

Existing general conventions for common objects 80

The Postal Union 81

The Institute of Agriculture 82

Eventual control of the League 83

    Note D.—List of societies 83

BOOK II.—The League in Being.

CHAPTER V.

THE CONSTITUTION OF THE LEAGUE.

Unexpected results of the war of 1914 87

Formation of the League of Nations 88

The Covenant and the official commentary (Art. 1) 89

No super-State 90

Members of the League 91

Joining members... 92

Withdrawal 94

xii CONTENTS.

CHAPTER V.—*continued.*

PAGE

Assembly and Council (Art. 2).............................. 95
Composition of Assembly 96
Selection of delegates free to every State 97
Meetings of Assembly; voting power (Art. 3) 98
Representation of British Empire 99
Meetings and powers 101
Composition of the Council (Art. 4) 101
Representation of new members and of specially
    interested Powers 104
Unanimity generally required: procedure (Art. 5) 105
Majority powers in exceptional cases 105
Agreement of members represented at meeting, why
    sufficient 107
Committee work 107
The Secretariat (Art. 6) 109
Why none for British Empire? 109
Seat of the League: appointments open to women
   (Art. 7).. 110

CHAPTER VI.

RESTRAINT OF WAR.

Armaments: plans for reduction: revision: private
    manufacture: exchange of information (Art. 8) ... 112
No compulsory disarmament 112
Failure of the Hague Conferences to deal with the
    problem 113
Future work of the Council.................................... 114
Private manufacture of war material 115
Modes of regulation 116
Prohibited means of offence: poison 117
The Commentary on exchange of information 119
Compulsory service not dealt with 120

Chapter VI.—*continued.*

PAGE

Advisory Commission on military, naval and air questions (Art. 9) 122

No General Staff created 123

Functions of the Commission 124

French position and proposed amendments 125

Integrity and independence of members to be preserved against external aggression (Art. 10) 127

Limits of guaranteed protection 128

Council must be unanimous in advice 128

No new Holy Alliance 129

Action in case of war or danger of war (Art. 11) 130

Importance of an instrument ready for action 132

CHAPTER VII.

JUDICIAL PROCESS AND SANCTIONS.

Agreement to submit disputes for arbitral award or inquiry by Council (Art. 12) 134

Reference of disputes to arbitration and performance of award (Art. 13) 135

Scope of discretion to refer questions 136

What questions justiciable 137

Choice of tribunal 138

Execution of award 138

Permanent Court to be established (Art. 14) 139

Composition of the Court 140

Competence 141

Submission of non-justiciable disputes to Council; power of Council to refer to Assembly (Art. 15)... 142

Possible use of committees 144

Publicity 145

Sanctions against war in breach of Covenant (Art. 16) 146

Commercial blockade of offending State 147

CHAPTER VII.—*continued.*

PAGE

" Pacific " blockade obsolete 148

Council has no compulsory power 149

Security for prompt co-operation to be desired 149

A cosmopolitan army not practicable 152

Proceedings as to States not members (Art. 17) 154

The League as general guardian of peace 155

CHAPTER VIII.

THE LEAGUE IN PEACE.

Registration of future treaties (Art. 18) 161

Revision of treaties, etc. (Art. 19) 162

General revision of law of nations 162

Obligations inconsistent with Covenant abrogated
  (Art. 20) 163

Saving of recognised engagements and understandings
  (Art. 21) 164

The Monroe Doctrine... 165

Mandates (Art. 22) 166

The Secretariat's duty 169

Co-operation in matters of labour, traffic, public health
  (Art. 23) 170

International commissions transferred to direction of the
  League (Art. 24)... 172

Red Cross work (Art. 25) 173

Amendments to the Covenant (Art. 26) 174

Annex (original members and invited States) 174

The spirit of the League 175

APPENDIX.

PAGE

I. The draft agreement for a League of Nations of
    Feb. 1919 177

II. The Covenant 189
     The Commentary... 204

III. The German scheme for a League of Nations 219

IV. The International Civil Court 231

V. The two branches of the Monroe Doctrine 235

VI. The Fourteen Points, etc. 237

THE LEAGUE OF NATIONS.

Book I.—INTRODUCTORY.

———◆———

CHAPTER I.

THE OLDER EUROPEAN ORDER.

References.

Du Bois, De recuperatione terre sancte: traité de politique générale par Pierre Du Bois, ed. Ch.-V. Langlois. Paris, 1891. Der Publizist Pierre Dubois . . . von Dr. Ernst Zeck. Berlin, 1911. Pierre Du Bois, légiste. In Renan's Etudes sur la politique religieuse du règne de Philippe le Bel (repr. from Histoire littéraire de la France). Paris, 1899.

St. Pierre, L'Abbé de St.-Pierre, sa vie et ses œuvres, par M. G. de Molinari. Paris, 1857.

E. Nys, Le droit international, ed. 1912, sect. 11, ch. 4: L'Arbitrage, vol. 2, p. 547: Le projet d'une cour internationale de justice, p. 577: see also the chapter "Les auteurs," vol. 1, pp. 224—351.

A. F. Pollard, The League of Nations in History (European alliances and the "Concert," 1815—1848). In collection of essays on the League of Nations. Oxford University Press, 1919.

Prof. Ramsay Muir, Nationalism and Internationalism. London, 1916. Section on "The Progress of Internationalism, 1815—1914," pp. 169—195.

Sir E. Satow, Guide to Diplomatic Practice. London, 1917.

————

WAR in one form or another is as old as any recorded history of mankind. The need of security in its double aspect of internal order and external defence has been the chief motive in the creation of States and Governments.

P.   1

In both cases, however, the ultimate object is peace. The strength of an established Government is shown not by frequent suppression of revolt, but by revolt having so little chance of success as to be infrequent; and success or failure in war is judged not so much by the immediate military advantage of the victor as by the relative permanence of the results. Alexander's conquests were greater in extent than those of any Roman commander, but he founded only a number of kingdoms unable to maintain peace among themselves; whereas the Empire which consolidated the conquests of the Roman republic assured peace to the civilised world for some centuries, a peace of which we are still reaping the fruits, in spite of that Empire's decline and fall.

Ever since the restoration of order in Europe which was accomplished in a tolerable though rude fashion in the early Middle Ages, men's thoughts have turned to the Roman peace and the problem of reviving its blessings by the prevention or restraint of war between civilised States. Mediæval speculation was still overshadowed by the dream of universal dominion. It was entangled from the thirteenth to the fifteenth century in an endless controversy between temporal and spiritual pretensions, and the Reformation, having brought about the definite repudiation of both imperial and papal authority by a great part of Christendom, made it finally manifest that this way was impossible.

Meanwhile peaceful settlement of disputes by reference to agreed arbitrations, a method which in private matters was far older than the establishment of regular courts of justice, was by no means unknown in public affairs. We have even, in the case of a difference between Henry II. of England and Philip II. of France, an exact precedent for the form of the twentieth-century arbitration on the Alaska boundary between Canada and the United States, namely the appointment by each party of three delegates (a). Reference to a single sovereign prince deemed to be impartial was, however, more frequent. Often that prince was the Pope (b): if he had not been a temporal ruler he might possibly have become the universal judge of national disputes by general consent and usage, and might have been a very good one. But, as it was, the materials for settling any kind of uniform practice did not exist, and there was no serious movement towards a general system of arbitration until the latter part of the nineteenth century.

From about 1500 at latest it was not only the fact, but an openly recognised fact, that Europe was divided into many kingdoms, principalities, and commonwealths, based no longer on real or fictitious kindred or on feudal allegiance, but on territorial control and jurisdiction, and that these independent units of political life did not own any common superior authority. As in theory it had always been allowed that war among civilised nations was a scandal (for the paradoxical position that war is rather a good thing in itself cannot vouch any ancient author to

(a) See Note A, p. 16.
(b) Sometimes the parties took the precaution of declaring that the reference was to the man by name as an individual, not to the Supreme Pontiff.

my knowledge), the question of finding some reasonable governance for the relations of independent Powers was now regarded as urgent by thinking men of divers nations. Sir Thomas More expressed the pious wish " that, whereas the most part of Christian princes be at mortal war, they were all at universal peace." That wish took shape in a line of speculation pursued from the sixteenth to the eighteenth centuries by several authors. Little visible fruit came of their labours at the time; nevertheless, they were the forerunners of the new movement aroused by the war of 1914, fostered by the zeal of leading publicists in Europe and in America, and at last embodied in the plan of the Paris Conference. Federal alliances in which the allied members committed matters of war and peace to some authority representing them all were already known to history; some were in actual being. Ancient Greece furnished examples in the Achæan League and, in an earlier rudimentary form, the Amphictyonic Council; the Swiss cantons were already secure in their collective independence; the United Provinces of the Netherlands were asserting theirs. Union had been compelled, in most of these cases, by the fear of some powerful aggressor against whom it was the only effectual means of resistance. At the same time it could be effectual only on condition of intestine strife between members of the alliance being forbidden; and thus evils less indeed than those of foreign conquest, but in themselves grave enough, were also prevented. Why should not the rulers of independent nations become parties to a compact of that kind for the avoidance of mutual strife at all times, and common defence if need

were; or even, the more ambitious projectors urged, for
a grand and final crusade of civilised Christendom to expel
infidel Powers from Europe and the Mediterranean?
Several plans of this kind were published and attracted
notice enough to earn a standing mention in text-books (c)
of international law somewhat later, when the subject had
reached the stage of having a recognised literature of its
own.   Among these projects the best known by name is
the Abbé de Saint-Pierre's; but our countryman, William
Penn's, earlier *Essay Towards the Present and Future
Peace of Europe* is of at least equal merit, and he appears
to have been the first writer who attacked the problem
with much practical sense of its conditions.   The conception of a congress of sovereign States "recognising no
earthly superior," with power to settle disputes by arbitration, was formed early in the fourteenth century, about
1306, by Pierre du Bois (d).   It is hard to tell exactly
how much importance Du Bois himself attached to this
point, or whether he knew what a great matter he was

(c) E. Nys, *Le droit international,* ed. 1912, is the most useful
I know for this purpose.   See also a summary list in Otlet,
Constitution mondiale de la société des nations, Geneva and Paris,
1917, p. 239.

(d) So I write the name, following Renan, whose essay, " Pierre
Du Bois, légiste," reprinted from the *Histoire littéraire de la
France* in " Etudes sur la politique religieuse du règne de
Philippe le Bel," Paris, 1899, is by no means superseded.   There
is now a critical edition of *De recuperatione terre sancte,* by
Ch.-V. Langlois, Paris, 1891; the old one is in *Liber secretorum
fidelium crucis,* uniform, and commonly found with and catalogued
as the second volume of, *Gesta Dei per Francos,* Hanover, 1611.
The latest monograph is by Dr. Ernst Zeck, *Der Publizist Pierre
Dubois,* Berlin, 1911.

touching. For he only touched it as one of a great
number of singularly bold and modern reforms, all of
which he represented as necessary preparation for a grand
crusade to be led by the King of France for the recon-
quest and settlement of the Holy Land. Abolition of the
Pope's temporal sovereignty,; wholesale confiscation and
redistribution of ecclesiastical property, including the
Templars' and Hospitallers' revenues, no contemptible bait
for Philip the Fair's avarice (e); application of such resources, among other objects, to training of interpreters for
the East, women as well as men, with medical and surgical
instruction thrown in—five centuries and more before the
days of our medical missions; a reformed summary and
uniform procedure for both civil and ecclesiastical jurisdiction, with short pleadings under the control of the
court; such are some of this fourteenth-century clerk's
innovations (f). No wonder that he never rose to high
office. It looks as if the great project of the crusade was
to his mind a desirable object (it would have been almost
heretical to deny that) to set before every Christian man,
but having a quite independent and (a scholar might hope)
less remote value as the vehicle of improvements in the
state of Christendom which, without some such powerful
impulse, could hardly make way against vested interests.

(e) But the French king was already devising his own shorter
way with the Temple: Du Bois' ink was hardly dry when he set
about it in such a fashion as made perhaps the blackest episode
in mediæval history. Du Bois was employed on this and other
occasions to write anti-Papal tracts, but not admitted to secrets
of State.

(f) References in Langlois' introduction, at pp. xvii.-xviii.

In any case the alliance Du Bois contemplated was not a
league of Christian princes on an equal footing, but a
confederation under the King of France as supreme leader.
There was even a suggestion of transferring the Empire
from the House of Hapsburg to the House of Valois.
Henri IV, of France's or Sully's project revived the same
design three centuries later; it was about as hopeful as
the opposite dream of the Protestant Powers allying themselves with the Grand Turk against the Papacy and the
Catholic princes, which indeed was more seriously considered (g).

It is true that neither William Penn's plan nor, so far
as I am aware, any other made any distinct provision for
• an executive authority to carry out the decrees of the
Diet or general assembly of the Powers.   Looked at in
the light of our modern experience this appears a very
serious omission.   But in the days of Marlborough's campaigns military preparations and movements were slow in
proportion to the imperfect state of all transport and communications, and the persons concerned in them were for
the most part too many for secrecy; so that the need for
prompt action in case of the terms of alliance being broken,
or a member of it attacked from without, was much less
obvious than it is now; not that all the framers or advocates of schemes for a league of peace have shown themselves alive to it even at this day.   Penn's foresight, at

(g) Something like it underlay the civilities exchanged by the
Sultan with Elizabeth and James I., of which the witness may be
seen in the Record Office Museum.   It found a strange advocate
in Jakob Böhme.

any rate, extended to a rough supervision of armaments. "If it be seen requisite, the question may be asked, by order of the sovereign States, why such a one either raises or keeps up a formidable body of troops, and he obliged forthwith to reform"—*i.e.*, in the French sense of disbanding then current in English—"or reduce them; lest any one, by keeping up a great body of troops, should surprise a neighbour."

All projects of this class, however, remained in the air; at most they gained words of praise from politicians who had no intention of acting upon them. Practical improvement (for, notwithstanding all exceptions and drawbacks, much improvement was effected) took place on other lines. The growth of the law of nations from the seventeenth to the twentieth century presents several marked stages. In the first of these it was recognised that there is a body of rules approved and received by the general usage of civilised nations as binding on their Governments in their dealings with one another, such rules not being confined to peaceful relations, but extending to the conduct of war. In point of fact the rules of war were earlier and in some ways better defined. Grotius holds, by common repute, the foremost place among the founders of the system; and, without prejudice to the merit of his precursors and successors, the common judgment is right. To this stage belongs the so-called doctrine of the Balance of Power or Balance of Europe (*h*), which in truth is little more than the moral of Louis XIV.'s conquests and even-

(*h*) These terms occur from the last quarter of the seventeenth onwards: Oxford English Dictionary, *s.v.* Balance, *sb.*, 13 *c*.

tual defeat. Any ruler who aims at preponderance in Europe may expect, and will deserve, to meet with a coalition of rivals and threatened lesser nations that will sooner or later be too strong for him. The lesson cannot be called obsolete; it had to be enforced not only once upon Louis XIV., but twice and thrice, after intervals of about a century, upon Napoleon and the Hohenzollerns, and in either case to the end of a swifter and more disastrous downfall. In the result the doctrine, or rather practical maxim, of the Balance of Power was a costly cure for the soaring ambition of despots, but not an effectual preventive. Kinglake, the historian of the Crimean War, tried to formulate a farther development in the shape of a "usage which tends to protect the weak against the strong." When wrong is done by a stronger to a weaker State, and some Great Power has a common interest with the weaker party, "then Europe is accustomed to expect" that Great Power to come to the rescue by diplomatic or armed intervention (i). No such rule, however, appears to have ever been officially recognised, nor is any trace of it to be found in text-books. Again, all rules and maxims are capable of abuse; honest but timid rulers may have found in the Balance of Power a source of anxiety and expense rather than security, and it is certain that unscrupulous ones could, and sometimes did, make it a pretext for their own aggressive designs. That is no reason nevertheless, for speaking of it with contempt, as if it belonged merely to the lumber of antiquated diplomatic

(i) *Invasion of the Crimea*, Vol. I., Ch. 2.

fictions, though it has been rather the fashion to do so of
late years. The principle was understood in a quite reasonable sense in the eighteenth century. Vauvenargues
sums it up neatly:—"La politique fait entre les princes
ce que les tribunaux de la justice font entre les par-
ticuliers: plusieurs faibles, ligués contre un puissant, lui
imposent la nécessité de modérer son ambition et ses
violences " (*k*).

On the whole, then, the European system of the eighteenth century, such as it was, made very little way
towards the prevention of war, and more or less widespread
wars were frequent. It was much, however, that customary rules were acknowledged to exist and were fairly
well observed.

The wars of the French Revolution and the greatness
and fall of Napoleon cleared the way for a second phase
of international relations. In 1814 and 1815 the proceedings at the Congress of Vienna were guided by the
five Great Powers, as they were now regularly called:
Austria, France, Great Britain, Prussia, and Russia; and
a moral duty to maintain peace in Europe on the foundation of the settlement then made was understood to rest
on those Powers. No regular method was provided for
securing agreement or resolving differences; the attempt
of the Continental monarchs to restore the old dynastic
system regardless of national aspirations was doomed to
failure from the outset; and yet, in a world tired out with
war, the arrangement was stable enough to give time for

(*k*) *Réflexions et Maximes*, No. 558.

recovery. There were local wars and warlike operations, revolutions, and civil strife of divers kinds, and in many parts of Europe, including a war between Russia and Turkey, not then counted as an European State; but forty years passed before there was an open and official rupture between Great Powers. As late as 1851 it was a common opinion that such a thing was hardly possible, and the revolutions of 1848 and 1849, in truth fatal symptoms of impending change, were deemed to have been passing disturbances. Louis Napoleon's ambition to found a dynasty and revive the glories of the first French Empire precipitated the ruin of the decaying order. One historian at least perceived clearly enough, looking back after some years, that the Crimean War had shattered the framework of the European system (l). Yet men's eyes were only half opened, both military art and diplomacy having in the main still followed the old ways.

From 1856 we may date a third period, marked in substance by the rise and consolidation of national States, absorbing or sweeping aside artificial divisions, and yet often accompanied by disregard for the claims of minorities; in form by endeavours to settle matters of common interest by special conferences and to restrain war within moderate limits of space when it could not be wholly avoided. Those immediate objects were in some measure attained: the latter wars of the third quarter of the nineteenth century were local, short, and decisive. Louis Napoleon's war of 1859 with Austria, producing a com-

(l) Kinglake, *op. cit., ad init.*

pleter effect than he desired, brought about the union of
Italy under the House of Savoy. Those of 1864 between
the old German confederation and Denmark, and of 1866
between Austria and Prussia with their respective German
allies, brought about exactly what Bismarck intended, the
virtual unity of Germany, excluding Austria, under Prussian supremacy; lastly the duel of France and Germany
in 1870 created the German Empire and, destroying the
Second Empire in France, made room for the third Republic. The visible results in Europe as compared with
those of eighteenth-century conflicts were, on the whole,
more considerable and less costly; it would take us too
far to consider the establishment of British supremacy in
India and North America. So far there was an appearance of improvement; unfortunately, the balance of good
and evil in those results was doubtful. Still guided by
antiquated precedent, the statesmen of Europe did not
perceive, or perceived too late, that they were working for
an unrivalled and unscrupulous master (m) of time and
opportunity, commanding the most formidable instrument
of land warfare yet known, the army created and trained
by the Prussian staff; and Bismarck, thus equipped in
arts and arms, and with Louis Napoleon's tortuous and
fumbling machinations playing into his hands, was working for the King of Prussia. That which no one could
help seeing after 1870 at latest was that the day of professional armies was over. Campaigns were no longer to
be conducted under artificial rules by leaders who hardly

(m) "A great man, but a great scoundrel," was Lord Acton's
colloquial estimate of Bismarck.

regarded one another as enemies, but rather as opposed advocates bound by a common tradition of professional courtesy. Henceforth conflicts in arms were to be the conflicts of whole nations, and the scale and burden of rival armaments rose without ceasing.

Before and in the course of the Crimean War attempts were made to settle the Eastern Question by diplomatic conferences of the Powers chiefly interested; and after the Congress (n) of Paris in 1856 there was a marked tendency to resort to conference of this kind as a means of quieting present or imminent disputes. Proposals to hold European conferences were not, however, always accepted; as to those which actually met, it might be rash to say positively that in any case war otherwise imminent was averted. A conference of plenipotentiaries may really settle a troublesome question, or may gain time for a more complete settlement by some transitory compromise, or may give the sanction of a formal treaty or declaration to changes known to all parties to be inevitable. The principal diplomatic congress of European Powers in our time was that of Berlin in 1878, where the terms of peace concluded between Russia and Turkey were revised with substantial alterations. It may happen that a conference

---

(n) " From the point of view of International Law there is no essential difference between Congresses and Conferences " (Sir E. Satow, *Guide to Diplomatic Practice,* ii., 1). Modern usage tends to reserve the higher title of Congress to meetings that aim at an extensive settlement. The term appears first in an identical phrase of the Treaties of Münster and Osnabrück, 1648: *op. cit.,* ii., 9. (See Chaps. 25, 26 *passim* for historical details and references.)

fails to agree and breaks up without any result having been attained. There are several examples of this before the nineteenth century; in our own days complete failure has been rare, but not unknown.

It would be unprofitable to speak in detail of the various diplomatic meetings of this period that were held with more or less adequate results, or, as sometimes happened, proposed but not held. An attempt to avert war between Russia and Turkey by this means, at the end of 1876, was unsuccessful; the Congress of Berlin, a year and a half later, did prevent the war from becoming general, and put off the evil day for thirty years. Still the settlement effected by the Treaty of Berlin was no better than a patching up. According to a careful judgment passed upon it in 1908, "it has not proved in any sense a' permanent settlement of an eternal question; it has not secured the peace of the Balkan peninsula; it has not ensured the just treatment of the Christian races which it left under Turkish rule" (o).

Within twenty years hostilities between Greece and Turkey had to be kept within bounds by the intervention of Great Powers; not all of them, for Germany and Austria soon stood aside, an omen of which few men saw the gravity at the time. Crete was pacified only by a series of acts not easily brought within any known category of international usage, but ultimately ratified by the consent or acquiescence of the Sultan (1897—1898). The final blow at the so-called Concert of Europe and the

(o) William Miller, *Cambridge Modern History*, xii., 399.

rather casual methods by which it worked was struck in 1908 by the Austro-Hungarian annexation of Bosnia and Herzegovina, with the support of Germany "in shining armour," as William II. boasted in a theatrical speech, and in flagrant contravention of the Treaty of Berlin. In form, but in form only, this high-handed act was afterwards legalised by a protocol concluded with the Turkish Government, on which the consent of the other Powers followed as of course (p).

Thus, in the two centuries and a half or thereabouts that have elapsed since the general recognition that there is a law of nations to be observed by civilised States in prin- ciple, in spite of all the drawbacks incident to imperfect definition and want of authentic jurisdiction, the political system of Europe has passed through the following stages. First, the competition and conflict of the eighteenth cen- tury, roughly moderated by the Balance of Power doctrine, and occasionally by more or less general and lasting agree- ments; next, the Vienna settlement guarded by the un- organised "concert" of the Great Powers so far as they could agree; then the period of national revival and of regulation, now considered a normal procedure, by special conferences; lastly, the redistribution of power in group alliances, accompanied by the increased vogue of arbitra- tion and the attempts of the Peace Conferences at The Hague to lay the foundations of a real international juris- diction. This last stage led immediately to the catastrophe

(p) Satow, *Guide to Diplomatic Practice*, § 101.

of the great war of 1914 and its unexpected and still uncertain consequences.

NOTE A.

The words of the treaty are as follows: Si autem super his quae excepta sunt [points of territorial dispute] per nosmet ipsos [in modern language, by ordinary diplomatic means] convenire non poterimus ego Philippus tres elegi episcopos et barones et ego Henricus totidem qui inter nos dicent et nos eorum iudicio stabimus firmiter et bona fide: Matth. Par., *Chron. Mai.*, ed. Luard, ii. 314. It is easy to suggest that the matter was an incidental boundary commission rather than an arbitration; but in any case the form is remarkable.

CHAPTER II.

METHODS OF INTERNATIONAL ARBITRATION.

References.

Lord Russell of Killowen, Address to the American Bar Association, 1896, L. Q. R. xii., at pp. 329, 330 (summary account of arbitration treaties down to that date), also at p. 333 (distinction between mediation or good offices and arbitration).

E. Nys, Le droit international, ed. 1912 (Brussels), vol. ii., pp. 534—77: Les solutions amiables des différends entre les Etats.

Sir Thomas Barclay, articles " Peace," " Peace Conferences," in Encyclopædia Britannica, 11th ed. List of standing arbitration treaties concluded down to 1910.

Solicitors' Journal, Nov. 1, 8, 1919. The antiquity of arbitration (ancient Greek examples).

REFERENCE to arbitrators was from ancient times a known and practised method of settling disputes between independent States. For whatever reason, it became much less common after the Middle ·Ages; perhaps because direct negotiation between the parties concerned was made more practicable by the institution of standing embassies and legations, and preferred by statesmen to formal argument. In the period on which we now enter we meet with a notable revival of the practice, coupled with serious endeavours to give it a systematic form.

First, resort to some kind of arbitral decision was stimulated by the example of Great Britain and the United States in settling a really dangerous controversy.

Then, early in the twentieth century, France and Great

P.   2

Britain concluded a treaty providing in general terms for
the reference of future disputes to arbitration, with the
exception of questions affecting national honour or vital
interests, and the pattern of this treaty was extensively
copied.

Meanwhile the Hague Conference of 1899 had made a
common form of arbitration treaty possible, and greatly
simplified the process of obtaining a decision, by creating
a standing judicial machinery of which governments that
were so minded might avail themselves at any time.

Endeavours were also made from time to time to devise
a form of international agreement that would cover all
disputes without exception.   Lately, after one or two
failures (*b*), Great Britain and the United States came
to such an agreement, in which the novel feature was the
consideration by a standing joint commission of cases not
found soluble by ordinary diplomatic means and not
thought capable of judicial treatment.   Several treaties
of this model, first settled in 1914, were soon afterwards
made between the United States and other nations.

All this, however, fell very far short of the establishment or recognition of a true judicial court administering
the law of nations with cosmopolitan authority.   Such a
court was the ideal of sanguine publicists, who hoped that
the civilized Powers of the world in congress might create
it and unanimously submit to its jurisdiction.   But German policy, at all times after the formation of the German

(*b*) A treaty of this type was also concluded between Italy
and the Argentine Republic in 1898, but not ratified: we need
not recur to it.

empire, was inflexibly opposed to the allowance of any
real international authority, professing to regard it as an
inadmissible derogation from the sovereign rights of an
independent State; and therefore nothing could be done
in that way. The reformers who were most zealous in
urging the proposals thus rejected were singularly blind
to the significance of the rejection.

Such is the historical outline which we shall now proceed
to fill in so far as appears necessary for the understanding
of the sequel. But first it may be well to make a few
remarks on the nature of arbitral tribunals and the difference between an arbitral award and on the one hand the
action of a mediator, on the other the judgment of a permanent court of justice; for erroneous assumptions and
exaggerated statements on this matter are not infrequent.

The functions of an arbitrator are so different from those
of a mediator that confusion ought not to be possible.
A mediator's business is to discuss the whole matter in
dispute with the parties and try to bring them together;
he is not bound to form any opinion of his own on its
merits, and if he does form one neither party is bound to
attend to it. He is to assist and advise, not to decide, and
his action is in no way judicial. The aim is not a declaration of right, but the settlement of a claim or of conflicting
claims, so that many reasons of expediency may quite
properly have weight which it would be quite improper
for an arbitrator acting judicially to consider. An arbitrator, on the contrary, is appointed to hear and determine
matters on which the parties have specifically declared
themselves to be at variance, and agreed to abide by his

2 (2)

decision. It may occur to him in the course of the proceedings, as it may occur to a judge, to suggest a compromise, but any such good offices are no part of his duty.
His business is to decide, not to advise, and he is bound to
proceed judicially and according to law—that is to say,
the law by which the parties have agreed to be bound; in
ordinary civil arbitrations this is presumed to be the law
of the land if nothing to the contrary is expressed.

As to the likeness and difference between an arbitrator
and a judge, we are not to think of them as belonging to
widely different species. An arbitrator is a person chosen
to act as judge on a particular occasion; the fact that his
authority is created by the parties and confined to the
occasion appears to constitute the specific character of the
office (c). There is no foundation for any notion that
he is less bound to observe the rules of judicial conduct
than the official judges of a permanent court. He may
not, for example, receive evidence that would not be admissible in a court of justice. It is doubtless true that, if
not learned in the law, he will be apt to put questions of
pure law in a subordinate rank as compared with his impression of the substantive merits. This, indeed, is usually
what the parties desire. Moreover, quite appreciable
variations of temperament and intellectual habit in this
respect are to be found even among the most learned
members of regular courts. It is also true that an arbitrator's jurisdiction is derived wholly from the consent of

(c) Cf. Baty, International Law, 1909, p. 8: " the acceptance
of a *persona grata* to decide a particular dispute."

the parties; they alone can define the question he has to decide, and they can, if they please, agree on a statement of the facts, or of specified points either of fact or of law, for the purpose of admitting the matters so agreed without discussion. But this difference is less material than it looks at first sight; for it must be remembered that, in the way of agreed statements or admissions and otherwise, parties to an ordinary civil litigation can do almost anything they choose by consent in English practice at any rate.

And generally there is no doubt that in our law arbitration is regarded as a known and proper kind of judicial process. Whatever else an arbitrator may or may not be, it is certain (speaking of the law and practice with which I am acquainted) that he is not an untrammelled dispenser of natural justice. As a normal result of the parties having put their special confidence in him, his award is not subject to any ordinary process of appeal, but can be set aside only on special grounds broadly reducible to bad faith, manifest error, and failure to dispose of the matters referred to arbitration; so that his findings of fact are less controllable than a jury's, and his rulings in law, express or tacit, are much less so than a judge's. Thus he has in fact a larger autonomy than a superior court. So have justices of the peace, and it is even said that judges of the High Court sometimes do things in chambers which are acquiesced in as convenient, but would be hard to justify if the point of jurisdiction were formally argued. None the less, all these ought to hear and determine according to law. Finally, an award is for most practical purposes as effectual and enforceable as a judgment of the proper court.

But, if an arbitrator is a kind of judge, his judgment-seat is not the seat of a permanent court, nor is he in the exercise of his office a member of such a court; and this is so even if he is a learned person and accustomed to regular judicial work. His jurisdiction is created for a special purpose and comes to an end when that purpose is fulfilled. His award has no authority beyond the particular occasion and the parties who have agreed to submit the dispute to him. This is the really vital difference between arbitration tribunals and a regular judicature, and we have to bear it in mind when we come to consider the League of Nations in its judicial aspect. We shall see that the Hague Convention did not establish a true court, but only provided a convenient mode of making up arbitral tribunals and regulating their procedure. Isolated awards of arbitrators or arbitral bodies, however conscientious and able, will not produce a coherent doctrine or settle any standing doubt. For those higher ends there is need of uniformity in method and continuity in practice and tradition, and these can be secured only at the judgment-seat of a permanent court. Moreover, although an arbitral award ought—in the view of English-speaking lawyers at any rate—to be founded on legal reasons, one cannot in fact always be sure what an arbitrator's reasons really were, especially in a case where the rule of law itself has never been adequately defined (a class to which, unfortunately, a considerable proportion of disputes between sovereign States belong). Accordingly, we may note in private affairs that when there occurs a serious disputable question of law between persons or bodies representing distinct and important interests, and the question or others allied to it seem likely to arise again, it is not thought enough to go to arbitration, but a test case is brought before a superior court for solemn argument and decision, and, it may be, carried up to the final appellate jurisdiction of the House of Lords, in order to obtain a decision binding for the future. But in the commonwealth of nations, in default of an established court having full judicial authority, no such course is possible at present. As between independent nations justice and judgment are still in the archaic stage of which we are reminded in the Iliad (d), where some kind of customary rule is recognized, but it can be administered only through the consent of parties to accept the decision of a man or body of men to whom they submit the cause of their own free will. In the Homeric age it seems to have been expected by public opinion that the family of a slain man should be willing to refer the amount of compensation to some respected elder or to the assembly, and in the years next before the war of 1914 the custom of civilized nations was thought by many publicists to have nearly if not quite reached a corresponding stage, with this advantage, that States which did elect to adopt judicial process could use all the learning and experience acquired during many centuries by courts and lawyers working in their respective local

(d) xvii., 497, the scene of a trial before elders described among the ornaments of Achilles' shield. See Dr. Leaf's note on the passage.

jurisdictions. The event showed that the Germans (not excluding learned ones) and the gods they worshipped were much behind the illiterate Achaians at the siege of Troy in wisdom and humanity, but strong enough to defy, with a show of success for some time, the resources of civilization available at the moment.

It may not be useless to deal here with some of the criticisms passed on arbitration as a general method of settlement, especially by certain continental jurists who belittle it in their zeal for a regular standing court, much as some years earlier certain champions of arbitration belittled all other methods. The merits have seldom been discussed in an impartial spirit. Advocates, of more zeal than discretion, have provoked opposition by claiming and expecting too much. They have represented arbitration and the Hague tribunal as a panacea; worse, they have committed themselves to ill-judged depreciation of other means to the same end, and in particular of official diplomacy. They have forgotten that the true success of diplomatic skill lies not in producing brilliant or convincing dispatches, but in checking incipient mischief at such an early stage that no dispatches have to be written. A few strictly confidential notes, to be disclosed only to a future generation, may be all the record of discussion and explanation which have dispersed a threatening war-cloud. Again, they have forgotten that, when men's temper is hot and calm judgment in abeyance, all means that serve to gain time are good, and none should be neglected. Moreover, they refused for a long time to be persuaded that not all disputes are equally fit subjects for judicial

treatment; but, inasmuch as the importance of distin-
guishing between justiciable and non-justiciable questions
is now generally recognized, there is no need to give more
than a passing mention to this error.

Contrariwise there has been exaggerated detraction,
partly founded on the extreme claims of pacifist authors.
It is absurd to complain of statesmen or arbitrators for not
being more nearly infallible than courts of justice, or of
arbitral awards for not satisfying all parties, when it is
notorious that the judgments of courts quite commonly
satisfy neither litigant. It is no less absurd to forget,
what we all have to remember in our particular jurisdictions, that the purpose of judicial proceedings is to render,
not incontrovertible decisions (for that is impossible to
human faculties), but decisions which at least are honest
and make a settlement good enough to be accepted as better
than strife.

There are also some critics, not without ability and influence, who openly deny more than a secondary importance to all and every one of the existing or projected instruments of pacific settlement. Man, they say, is a com-
bative animal. Nations and communities have always
had conflicting interests and always will; they have always
fought for them and therefore always will. This line of
argument sends us back in imagination to the first sitting
of the first court—wherever and whenever it may have been
—that exercised compulsory jurisdiction. One sees a little
group of elders who stand aside and shake their wise heads.
This new-fangled coercion, they say, will never do.
Voluntary submission to an award and voluntary compen-

sation according to the award are doubtless to be encouraged with discretion; but beware of laying profane
experimental hands on the ultimate right of resort to the
blood-feud. It is a venerable and sacred institution
handed down by our valiant ancestors, bound up with the
very life of the clan and the family. When you begin to
meddle with it you are in peril of shaking the foundations
of society before you have done. Social order rests on the
honour, independence, and vital interests of kindred
groups. Your compulsory jurisdiction is the first step on
the road to anarchy. Besides, public opinion is already
declaring itself in favour of submission and composition in
proper cases. The head of a house who will not hear of
compounding an ordinary feud, such as arises from a clean
manslaying in fair fight, is coming to be looked on as a
bad neighbour. Leave it there, and you will have all practicable improvement without laying down hard and fast
rules to make occasions for new strife. So, doubtless, those
elders argued; but they did not prevail, and for some
thousand years compulsory justice has been recognized
among the necessary attributes of civilized government.

One might even go farther back in the struggle of pre-
historic reformers, and strain the mind's ear to catch the
muttering of sage reproof against the first farmer who
dared to harness a horse to his plough; or, before him, the
more daring one who tamed the first ox-team, discarding
his ancestral spade; not to mention the yet bolder inno-
vators, far beyond the reach of conjecture, who sowed the
first corn and made fire to light the first hearth. Were
they stoned or deified—or both? Tubal Cain, following

on Prometheus, is a symbol of forgotten controversy. There must have been champions of the Stone Age who fought hard for the old ways, and it is not without reason that iron, having won the day, is still deemed a potent counter-charm against the more ancient magic. But let us return to the doubters of our present epoch.

Those who affect to despair of the peace of nations are, we believe, for the most part honest in their pessimism. Some are born pessimists in all affairs, their own as well as the nation's. Others become pessimists from having been unsuccessful reformers. Others again are consciously sincere, but unconsciously biassed by their private interests and associations. That kind of bias is a serious element in the problem. It may become less dangerous when the world finds, as it will very soon, that beating swords into ploughshares, not in a metaphorical but in a quite material sense, with no figure of speech beyond putting part for a greater whole, is anything but unprofitable. Admirals and generals, perhaps, cannot be expected to find much comfort in the reflection that even if all wars could instantly cease by a miracle we should still have ample use for the virtues of naval and military discipline in many forms of peaceful adventure and enterprise, exploring expeditions, world organizations of industry and so forth; nevertheless it is obviously true.

Sometimes it is alleged as a defect in international as compared with private arbitration that the arbitrators have no settled rule of law to guide them (e). The root of this

(e) " Les arbitres ne sont en possession d'aucune loi à appliquer ": Otlet, Constitution mondiale de la société des nations, 1917, p. 13.

objection appears to be the timid and narrow doctrine of judicial interpretation which has been common, though not without weighty protest, on the continent of Europe. It is assumed that in the absence of an express formula, covering the case in hand a judge, and therefore an arbitrator likewise, is helpless. Our English and American tradition is quite otherwise: for we hold that the first commandment of the law is to judge according to reason; not any and every man's uninformed reason, but reason instructed by the experience of many generations and embodied in positive rules and accepted principles, yet so that, if no binding authority can be produced, or authorities are conflicting, it is still the judge's duty to find the most reasonable solution he can. Any one who imagines that such a problem is unknown or uncommon within the sphere of municipal law must be very little acquainted with the jurisprudence of his own or any other country. We may observe, as a matter of detail not wholly irrelevant, that national courts have before them from day to day cases of increasing number and importance in which the most troublesome question is which of two or more legal systems brought into competition by the special facts is to furnish the court with the rule to be applied. Cases of "the first impression" on the one hand, where the field lies open to judicial reason; cases of "conflict of laws" on the other hand, where a definite choice between competing rules has to be made; both kinds may be difficult, but neither of them presents unknown terrors to a properly trained English-speaking lawyer.

Now let us ask whether an international tribunal is really at an enormous disadvantage in the matter of guiding principles. In the first place it is always open to the parties themselves to define beforehand the rules they will accept as binding. This was done in the *Alabama* case and might well be done again. If not, the arbitrators have to decide according to the general law of nations and such applicable obligations as may have been formulated in treaties or conventions to which the litigants were contracting parties. And what is the general law of nations? cries the sceptical pessimist: only a mass of assertions and opinions backed by no sanction and controlled by no authentic interpretation.—Here we must insist on keeping out the standing problem of sanctions, for it is in no way to the purpose. It is inconvenient not to know how a rule can be enforced, but that is quite a different kind of inconvenience from not knowing what the rule is. In fact the contrast in point of certainty between municipal and international law has been much exaggerated. There is no system of law, codified or uncodified, in which one may not find many unsettled questions, if only because new questions must arise from time to time, but there are plenty of other causes.

More than this, there is no system in which discussion of an unsettled question, however learned and elaborate, can be confidently expected to lead to a clear solution in every case. Decisions between parties often turn on special matters of fact or on questions of law collateral to the main governing principles. In the Common Law we have judgments that seem, as we turn the pages of the report, on the very point of clearing away doubts, explaining ambiguous authorities, and overruling erroneous ones, and then wilfully stop short of a final conclusion. All of us who have seriously worked at the more general problems of our case law have pondered over such judgments with mixed admiration and regret. There is such a thing as being too astute to observe the rule, a sound rule in itself, of deciding no more than is required for disposing of the matter in hand. Subject to the correction of French colleagues, I believe as much may be said with truth of the body of doctrine which labours partly judicial and partly academic have built on the foundation of the Napoleonic codes. It is not in the nature of legal science to be reducible to a series of demonstrated and authentic propositions applicable to all possible questions that may come into court.

But this does not mean that reasonable certainty is not attainable as to the rules governing the majority of questions that have in fact to be disposed of. Now if we look to the subject-matter of international arbitrations, as far as experience has gone, we shall find that a notable proportion of them, something near one-third, have been concerned with matters of territorial title in the form of boundary disputes and other questions of a like sort. It so happens that international law has no lack of rules for dealing with such claims, and that, being in the main founded on the classical Roman law of property, they are fairly well settled. As in municipal law, the difficulties are apt to be not so much in the law as in the facts. Thus in the Guiana boundary difference between Great Britain, deriving title from Holland, and Venezuela, deriving title from Spain, there was no principle of law nor of general usage in dispute. Not legal but historical uncertainty made the decision troublesome; the territory in question was for the most part unsettled, and the evidence of any continuous or effective possession under either Spanish or Dutch jurisdiction was anything but full or satisfactory. Thus, again, the case of the Bering Sea fisheries between Great Britain and the United States was of the first impression. The facts, and the claims of property and jurisdiction arising from them, were wholly novel.

One common source of difference, occurring both in territorial claims and in other kinds of dispute, is in the construction of treaties. Here it cannot be said that guidance is wanting. Apart from the technical effect of particular terms in this or that system, the main principles of interpretation are common to all civilized law, and the resources of jurisprudence and of historical criticism are no less open to arbitrators than to any other serious inquirer. It may happen that the parties have appointed ignorant and incompetent persons; in that case it is the parties' own fault.

Another charge made against international arbitrators is that their awards are too often in the nature of a compromise. On this I shall only remark that jurymen are also ministers of justice and sworn to give a true verdict according to the evidence; they are bound to attend only to legally admissible evidence, and to follow the Court's directions in point of law, and there are defined rules of law about the measure of damages. But in fact nobody doubts that verdicts in many cases, and the assessment of damages in more, are the result of compromise between a majority and a more or less obstinate minority. Our courts have wisely refused to inquire by what process

verdicts are arrived at, though there are limits beyond
which the jury's freedom of aberration may be restrained.
Even the reasons given by the Judicial Committee of the
Privy Council for its advice to the King, which have to
be expressed in one collective opinion by force of a rule
not originally framed with a view to any judicial functions, often represent not the whole mind of the framer
but only so much of it as he could induce his colleagues on
the Board or an effective majority of them to accept.

Lastly, we have to bear in mind that an arbitral tribunal, as distinct from a permanent court, is just what
the parties choose to make it. Using or not using the panel
of judges and the procedure provided by the Peace Conferences, they can have a tribunal composed wholly of
jurists, or including diplomatists or persons who, being
neither jurists nor diplomatists, are specially qualified by
knowledge of the subject-matter. If they want a strictly
legal court they can have it; if they want a board of
specialists, surveyors it may be, or naval or military men,
they can have it; if they please they may combine all or
any of these elements. Probably the last thing that occurs
to them is the satisfaction of those learned persons who
look on national interests and differences as material for
the production of such neat academic formulas as learned
persons may with the least trouble to themselves work
into a neat and elegant system.

The first notable example of arbitration being applied
to a serious dispute between great nations in modern times
was the *Alabama* case, as it is commonly called. A composite arbitral tribunal sitting at Geneva in 1871 and 1872

fixed the liability of Great Britain to the United States
for damage done by vessels which had escaped from British
ports during the American Civil War and been equipped
elsewhere as Confederate cruisers (f). This was by no
means the first arbitral award between the two English-
speaking Powers, but none of the former ones had been
of comparable importance. Accordingly this became a
leading example, and may be said to have given a decisive
impulse to international arbitration in the last quarter of
the nineteenth century, notwithstanding that the proceedings cannot be regarded as a satisfactory model, and have
never been imitated in detail. The labours of the tribunal
were lightened, and indeed made possible, by the parties
having defined beforehand, in the Treaty of Washington,
the rules to be applied; those rules laid down a neutral
State's duty of diligence to prevent its territory being
made a base of warlike operations, and the terms were
wide enough to amount in effect to an admission of some
liability on the British side. It would not be to our
purpose here to recall the particulars. There was much
disapproval of the result in England, and there is no
doubt that the damages awarded were excessive, inasmuch
as there ultimately remained in the treasury of the United
States a balance for which no claimants were forthcoming.
Nothing came of a suggestion that the rules embodied in
the treaty should be accepted by other States as part of
the conventional law of nations; but, apart from any ques-

(f) The statement of the facts in Enc. Laws of England, *s.v.*
Alabama case, is correct only as to the *Florida*, not as to the
Alabama, whose evasion was due to an unfortunate accident.

P.   3

tion of wording, the principle that there is some duty of
reasonable diligence does not appear to be now seriously
disputed. Neither can it be doubted that this case, like
sundry other leading cases in a more strictly professional
sphere with which English-speaking lawyers are familiar,
has enjoyed a reputation and acquired a value as a precedent altogether beyond the questions actually decided
and the reasons, expressed or not expressed, of the decision.

After Great Britain and the United States had demonstrated the possibility of settling a grave question between
sovereign States in this manner, notwithstanding that on
both sides feeling ran high, that there were incidents in
the very course of the proceedings not calculated to appease
it, and that the composition of the tribunal was in some
ways not felicitous, arbitration was restored to all and
more than all its mediæval repute, and frequently applied
with improved methods and procedure.

Various ways of constituting an arbitral tribunal are
possible and have been used in recent times. It cannot
be said that the practice showed any tendency to uniformity, save that in every case where a composite court
has been formed it has contained representatives of each
party. Arbitrations having this feature in common have
presented three distinct variations. The tribunal may be
reinforced by members whom foreign, and presumably
impartial, rulers nominate on the request of the parties;
or by an external member agreed on by the parties' representatives; or it may not be reinforced at all. Examples
of the first method are the *Alabama* case, and, in a better
shape, the Bering Sea arbitration of 1893. The second

was used in the Guiana boundary arbitration, which settled a long-drawn dispute between Great Britain and Venezuela in 1899. In the matter of the Alaska boundary, disposed of in 1903, there were three members appointed by the United States and three by Great Britain and Canada. The risk of an equal division is an obvious objection to this plan; in the particular case the American and Canadian members voted for their own sides, and if the British arbitrator, Lord Alverstone, had done the same there would have been a deadlock. His judicial opinion, however, was against the Canadian case, and there was unpleasant and undignified complaint in Canada, though learned Canadians were not wanting who had the courage and candour to say that he was right. We do not think this procedure is likely to be repeated. Under the Hague Conventions the tribunal is normally made up of four members, two selected by each party, and a fifth nominated as umpire by the four; but in the most important case since 1907, that of the North Atlantic Coast Fisheries in 1909-10, the parties came to a direct agreement as to all the members (*g*).

At the same time the ancient method of reference to the judgment of some one foreign ruler, or a high official of a foreign State, was by no means extinct. It was applied more than a dozen times in the second half of the nineteenth century (*h*). Perhaps the most striking example

(*g*) The Hague Court Reports, New York, 1916, p. 185.

(*h*) Encycl. Brit., 11th ed., ii., 329, *s.v.* Arbitration, International. The case of Chile and Argentina mentioned in the text is omitted by some accident in this table.

is the settlement of the boundary dispute between Chile and Argentina by the award of King Edward VII. in 1902; the choice of such an arbitrator might perhaps have been resented in the United States as coming under the somewhat elastic description of European interference with American affairs, but for the cordial relations produced by the attitude of Great Britain in the Spanish-American War.

The more general type of arbitration treaties which has become common since Great Britain and France concluded the first of the kind in 1903 (*i*) provides for reference to the permanent Court of Arbitration established at the Hague under the Convention of 1899. It also requires a preliminary agreement (*compromis*) (*k*) defining the matter in dispute and the terms of the reference. In the treaties to which the United States is a party it is further expressed that this " special agreement " will be made by the President of the United States " by and with the advice and consent of the Senate thereof ": the Senate would allow standing arbitration treaties only on this condition, holding that the special agreement is itself in the nature of a treaty (*l*), and being exceedingly jealous as to the full preservation of its constitutional rights in foreign affairs. Great Britain in turn reserves the right to consult the governments of self-governing Dominions before conclud-

(*i*) See the text in Note B at the end of this chapter.

(*k*) The French word for the English " compromise " is " transaction "; this difference of idiom is a rather common stumbling-block of the less competent sort of translators.

(*l*) In fact the special agreement in the North Atlantic Coast Fisheries case was an elaborate instrument of eleven articles.

ing an agreement to refer a difference in any matter specially affecting their interests. About one hundred general arbitration treaties, presumably in almost identical terms, were in force before the outbreak of war in 1914 (*m*).

It was a pretty common opinion both before and after the Peace Conference of 1899 that the ideal of an arbitration treaty covering all possible disputes without exception could not be attained, at any rate as between Great Powers (*n*), within any assignable time. Such an undertaking appeared to be imprudent; there might be situations, it seemed, in which the rulers of a nation—remembering that after all they are not owners but trustees—could not properly commit their cause to the judgment of any tribunal, even one in the appointment of which they themselves had an equal share. But there were those, especially in America, who sought a more excellent way. Without denying that in principle "justiciable" questions —namely, such as can be brought to a definite issue and handled in a judicial manner—are materially different from those called "non-justiciable," or political as involving matters of policy not reducible to any legal measure, they observed that the method of formal argument and decision is not necessarily the only one capable of leading

(*m*) Ninety were communicated to the permanent office of the Hague tribunal down to 1910: Nys, Le droit international, ed. 1912, ii., 566.

(*n*) Such treaties were in fact made by Denmark with the Netherlands in 1904, Italy in 1905, and Portugal in 1907: 2me Conf. intern. de la paix, Actes et documents, ii., 887.

to a settlement.   Joint commissions appointed by two
governments to examine and report on matters in doubt,.
such as details of boundaries in imperfectly surveyed territory, or even to decide points of detail, were already well
known.   Indeed, their work had not been confined to minor
questions.   For example, such a commission had framed
the Treaty of Washington, which was the really decisive
step in the quieting of the *Alabama* controversy.   Could
not this method be extended and made permanent so as
to secure a calmer and more deliberate investigation than
is possible in the ordinary diplomatic exchange of communications?   A mixed commission having no power to
do anything but inquire and report will at least be less
subject to friction and the heat that comes of friction than
Foreign Secretaries writing controversial dispatches to one
another with an eye to their appearance in an official collection.   Danger of controversial deadlock can be still
further lessened by appointing the Commissioners as a
standing body and not waiting till a dispute has actually
arisen.

Such, it is presumed, were the considerations that led
to the framing of the British-American treaty signed at
Washington in September and ratified in November 1914,
purporting to be not an arbitration treaty but " with
regard to the establishment of a peace commission."   It
would serve no useful purpose to give more than bare mention here to a somewhat earlier draft which was signed but
not ratified.   The treaty (*o*) does not abrogate the earlier

(*o*) 1914, Cd. 7714, reprinted in Note O at the end of this
chapter.

convention providing for reference to the Hague tribunal, but sets up a permanent international commission to which disputes " of every nature whatsoever " between the contracting parties not settled under existing agreements " shall, when diplomatic methods of adjustments have failed, be referred for investigation and report "; pending which there shall be no hostilities (Art. 1).

To make up the standing Commission, each government chooses one countryman of its own and one foreigner; a fifth, not being a citizen of either contracting party, is chosen by agreement (Art. 2). These appointments were in fact made in due course. Special provision is made for the representation of the Dominion governments in proper cases. The Commission may offer its services of its own motion. A year is allowed for inquiry and report. The High Contracting Parties expressly reserve their subsequent freedom of action.

Treaties of the same model have since been concluded by the United States to the number, it is said, of about thirty. They are often referred to as the Bryan treaties, Mr. Bryan having been Secretary of State when the first of them was made. A desire to advance the cause of general peace is expressly mentioned in the original treaty as one of the reasons for making it; and, considering that a general European war had actually begun when it was signed, the multitude of imitators is remarkable. We need hardly say that this form of agreement, even more than the earlier limited arbitration treaties, assumes the existence and continuance on both sides of good faith and a sincere desire to avoid war. A State whose rulers hold that the obligation of treaties is overridden by so-called military necessity, or even by the prospect of military advantage, will observe a treaty providing for reference of disputes to an arbitrator for award or to a joint commission for report, or for putting off the outbreak of hostilities in any way whatever, just as much and as little as any other agreements—that is, so far and so far only as the rulers find their profit therein; a profit which they will call national as a matter of course, but it may well enough be only dynastic or personal. Thus the destroyed empire of Austria-Hungary had really no common national interest at all.

NOTE B.

I. Agreement between the United Kingdom and France providing for the Settlement by Arbitration of certain classes of questions which may arise between the two Governments.

Signed at London, October 14, 1903.

The Government of His Britannic Majesty and the Government of the French Republic, signatories of the Convention for the pacific settlement of international disputes, concluded at the Hague on the 29th July, 1899;

Taking into consideration that by Article XIX of that Convention the High Contracting Parties have reserved to themselves the right of concluding Agreements, with a view to

Le Gouvernement de Sa Majesté Britannique et le Gouvernement de la République Française, signataires de la Convention pour le règlement pacifique des conflits internationaux conclue à La Haye le 29 Juillet 1899;

Considérant que, par l'Article XIX de cette Convention, les Hautes Parties Contractantes se sont réservé de conclure des accords en vue du recours à l'arbitrage, dans tous les cas referring to arbitration all questions which they shall consider possible to submit to such treatment,

Have authorized the Undersigned to conclude the following arrangement:—

ARTICLE I.

Differences which may arise of a legal nature, or relating to the interpretation of Treaties existing between the two Contracting Parties, and which it may not have been possible to settle by diplomacy, shall be referred to the Permanent Court of Arbitration established at the Hague by the Convention of the 29th July, 1899, provided, nevertheless, that they do not affect the vital interests, the independence, or the honour of the two Contracting States, and do not concern the interests of third Parties.

ARTICLE II.

In each individual case the High Contracting Parties, before appealing to the Permanent Court of Arbitration, shall conclude a special Agreement defining clearly the matter in dispute, the scope of the powers of the Arbitrators, and the periods to be fixed for the formation of the Arbitral Tribunal and the several stages of the procedure.

qu'elles jugeront possible de lui soumettre,

Ont autorisé les Soussignés à arrêter les dispositions suivantes:—

ARTICLE I.

Les différends d'ordre juridique ou relatifs à l'interprétation des Traités existant entre les deux Parties Contractantes qui viendraient à se produire entre elles, et qui n'auraient pu être réglés par la voie diplomatique, seront soumis à la Cour Permanente d'Arbitrage établie par la Convention du 29 Juillet 1899 à La Haye, à la condition toutefois qu'ils ne mettent en cause ni les intérêts vitaux ni l'indépendance ou l'honneur des deux États Contractants, et qu'ils ne touchent pas aux intérêts de tierces Puissances.

ARTICLE II.

Dans chaque cas particulier, les Hautes Parties Contractantes, avant de s'adresser à la Cour Permanente d'Arbitrage, signeront un compromis spécial, déterminant nettement l'objet du litige, l'étendue des pouvoirs des Arbitres et les délais à observer, en ci qui concerne la constitution du Tribunal Arbitral et la procédure.

ARTICLE III.	ARTICLE III.
The present Agreement is concluded for a period of five years, dating from the day of signature.	Le présent Arrangement est conclu pour une durée de cinq années à partir du jour de la signature.
Done in duplicate at London, the 14th day of October, 1903.	Fait à Londres, en double exemplaire, le 14 Octobre 1903.

(L.S.) LANSDOWNE.
(L.S.) PAUL CAMBON.

II. CONVENTION OF 1908 BETWEEN GREAT BRITAIN AND THE UNITED STATES.

HIS Majesty the King of the United Kingdom of Great Britain and Ireland and of the British Dominions beyond the Seas, Emperor of India, and the President of the United States of America, desiring in pursuance of the principles set forth in Articles 15—19 of the Convention for the pacific settlement of international disputes, signed at The Hague July 29, 1899, to enter into negotiations for the conclusion of an Arbitration Convention, have named as their Plenipotentiaries, to wit:

His Majesty the King of the United Kingdom of Great Britain and Ireland and of the British Dominions beyond the Seas, Emperor of India, The Right Honourable James Bryce, O.M., and

The President of the United States of America, Elihu Root, Secretary of State of the United States,

Who, after having communicated to one another their full powers, found in good and due form, have agreed on the following articles:

ARTICLE 1.

[Identical with Art. 1 of the agreement of 1903 between the United Kingdom and France, see above.]

ARTICLE 2.

In each individual case the High Contracting Parties, before appealing to the Permanent Court of Arbitration, shall conclude a special Agreement defining clearly the matter in dispute, the scope of the powers of the Arbitrators, and the periods to be fixed for the formation of the Arbitral Tribunal and the several stages of the procedure. It is understood that such special agreements on the part of the United States will be made by the President of the United States, by and with the advice and consent of the Senate thereof; His Majesty's Government reserving the right before concluding a special agreement in any matter affecting the interests of a self-governing Dominion of the British Empire to obtain the concurrence therein of the Government of that Dominion.

Such Agreements shall be binding only when confirmed by the two Governments by an Exchange of Notes.

ARTICLE 3.

The present Convention shall be ratified by His Britannic Majesty, and by the President of the United States of America by and with the advice and consent of the Senate thereof. The ratifications shall be exchanged at Washington as soon as possible, and the Convention shall take effect on the date of the exchange of its ratifications.

ARTICLE 4.

The present Convention is concluded for a period of five years, dating from the day of the exchange of its ratifications.

Done in duplicate at the City of Washington, this fourth day of April, in the year 1908.

> (Signed) JAMES BRYCE.
> (Signed) ELIHU ROOT.

NOTE C.

TREATY BETWEEN THE UNITED KINGDOM AND THE UNITED STATES OF AMERICA WITH REGARD TO THE ESTABLISHMENT OF A PEACE COMMISSION.

Signed at Washington, September 15, 1914.

[*Ratifications exchanged at Washington, November* 10, 1914.]

HIS Majesty the King of the United Kingdom of Great Britain and Ireland and of the British Dominions beyond the Seas, Emperor of India, and the President of the United States of America, being desirous to strengthen the bonds of amity that bind them together and also to advance the cause of general peace, have resolved to enter into a Treaty for that purpose, and to that end have appointed as their Plenipotentiaries:—

His Britannic Majesty: The Right Honourable Sir Cecil Arthur Spring-Rice, G.C.V.O., K.C.M.G., &c., His Ambassador Extraordinary and Plenipotentiary at Washington; and

The President of the United States: The Honourable William Jennings Bryan, Secretary of State of the United States;

Who, after having communicated to each other their respective full powers, found to be in proper form, have agreed upon and concluded the following articles:—

ARTICLE 1.

The High Contracting Parties agree that all disputes between them, of every nature whatsoever, other than disputes the settlement of which is provided for and, in fact, achieved under existing agreements between the High Contracting Parties, shall, when diplomatic methods of adjustment have failed, be referred for investigation and report to a Permanent International Commission, to be constituted in the manner prescribed in the next succeeding article; and they agree not to declare war or begin hostilities during such investigation and before the report is submitted.

ARTICLE 2.

The International Commission shall be composed of five members, to be appointed as follows:—

One member shall be chosen from each country by the Government thereof; one member shall be chosen by each Government from some third country; the fifth member shall be chosen by common agreement between the two Governments, it being understood that he shall not be a citizen of either country.

The expenses of the Commission shall be paid by the two Governments in equal proportions.

The International Commission shall be appointed within six months after the exchange of the ratifications of this Treaty, and vacancies shall be filled according to the manner of the original appointment.

ARTICLE 3.

In case the High Contracting Parties shall have failed to adjust a dispute by diplomatic methods, they shall at once refer it to the International Commission for investigation and report. The International Commission may, however, spontaneously, by unanimous agreement, offer its services to that effect, and in such case it shall notify both Governments and request their co-operation in the investigation.

In the event of its appearing to His Majesty's Government that the British interests affected by the dispute to be investigated are not mainly those of the United Kingdom, but are mainly those of some one or more of the self-governing dominions, namely, the Dominion of Canada, the Commonwealth of Australia, the Dominion of New Zealand, the Union of South Africa, and Newfoundland, His Majesty's Government shall be at liberty to substitute as the member chosen by them to serve on the International Commission for such investigation and report another person selected from a list of persons to be named, one for each of the self-governing dominions, but only one shall act—namely, that one who represents the dominion immediately interested.

The High Contracting Parties agree to furnish the Permanent International Commission with all the means and facilities required for its investigation and report.

The report of the International Commission shall be completed within one year after the date on which it shall declare its investigation to have begun, unless the High Contracting Parties shall limit or extend the time by mutual agreement. The report shall be prepared in triplicate; one copy shall be presented to each Government and the third retained by the Commission for its files.

The High Contracting Parties reserve the right to act independently on the subject-matter of the dispute after the report of the Commission shall have been committed.

ARTICLE 4.

This Treaty shall not affect in any way the provisions of the Treaty of the 11th January, 1909, relating to questions arising between the United States and the Dominion of Canada.

ARTICLE 5.

The present Treaty shall be ratified by His Britannic Majesty and by the President of the United States of America, by and with the advice and consent of the Senate thereof, and the ratifications shall be exchanged at Washington as soon as possible. It shall take effect immediately after the exchange of ratifications, and shall continue in force for a period of five years, and it shall thereafter remain in force until twelve months after one of the High Contracting Parties have given notice to the other of an intention to terminate it.

In witness whereof the respective Plenipotentiaries have signed the present Treaty and have affixed thereunto their seals.

Done in duplicate at Washington on the fifteenth day of September, in the year of Our Lord nineteen hundred and fourteen.

(L.S.)   CECIL SPRING-RICE.
(L.S.)   WILLIAM JENNINGS BRYAN.

CHAPTER III.

THE HAGUE TRIBUNAL.

References.

[The Acts and Conventions of the Peace Conferences have been several times reprinted; the discussions are fully reported only in the official editions published by the Government of the Netherlands.]

Officially published by the Government of the Netherlands: Conférence internationale de la paix. The Hague, 1899 (four parts separately paged). Deuxième conférence internationale de la paix, Actes et documents. The Hague, 1907. 3 Vols. (in fact issued 1908-9).

International documents, ed. E. A. Whittuck. London, 1908. (Includes Declaration of Paris, 1856; Geneva Convention, 1864, and supplements, &c.; as well as the Hague Conventions.)

Les conventions et déclarations de la Haye de 1899 et de 1907, &c., avec une introduction de James Brown Scott. New York (Carnegie Endowment), 1918. Authentic French texts of 1899 and 1907 in parallel columns; full statement in tabular form and otherwise of the several Powers' ratifications, reservations, &c.

North Atlantic Coast Fisheries Arbitration at the Hague: argument on behalf of the United States by Elihu Root, ed. Robert Bacon and James Brown Scott. Cambridge, Mass. (Harvard University Press), 1917. Full account of the procedure at pp. xxv. *sqq.*

The proceedings in this arbitration were printed at large by the British Foreign Office, 1909-1910, 4 vols. fo., and by the Government of the United States, 1912-1913, 12 vols. 8vo.

The Hague Court Reports, comprising the awards, and other documents in each case submitted to the permanent court of arbitration and to commissions of inquiry; edited with an introduction by James Brown Scott. New York, &c. (Oxford University Press), 1916.

James Brown Scott, Une cour de justice internationale. New York (Carnegie Endowment), 1918. A consolidated version in French of the two volumes by the same writer, entitled: Letter and Memorandum of January 12, 1914, to the Netherlands Minister of Foreign Affairs, in behalf of the establishment of an International Court of Justice (1916); The Status of the International Court of Justice, &c. (1916).

Wehberg, Hans, The Problem of an International Court of

Justice, translated by Charles G. Fenwick.   Oxford, &c.
(Carnegie Endowment), 1918.

   Schücking, Walther, The international union of the Hague
Conferences, translated from the German [published in 1912]
by Charles G. Fenwick.   1918 (Carnegie Endowment, as above).

   Roland Gray, International tribunals in the light of the history
of law.   Harvard Law Review, May, 1919 (xxxii., 825).

WE now have to consider the judicial machinery provided
by the Hague Conventions and accepted in the typical
arbitration treaties of the last fifteen years or thereabouts.
The original promoter of the Peace Conferences was
Nicolas II., the late and to present seeming the last
Emperor of Russia, whose predecessor Alexander I. had
thrown out vague suggestions directed to the same end
almost a century earlier.   Of Alexander it may be said
that only steadfast purpose was lacking to make him
capable of being a great and beneficent ruler; nor is there
any cause to doubt that Nicolas, a much weaker man,
acted under a sincerely generous impulse.   When he issued
his appeal to the civilized world through the representatives of their governments at Petrograd, he regarded some
way of checking excessive armaments as the first aim of
the Conference.   But when, almost exactly twenty years
ago (a), the government of the Netherlands had assembled
the delegates of all the Great Powers and many of the
lesser ones at the Hague in compliance with the Tsar's
request, it appeared that no practical limitation of armaments was likely to be devised in any form generally
acceptable, or to be accepted at all by Germany in par-

(a) May 18th, 1899.

ticular; and the total results would have been disappoint-
ing had not the exertions of Lord Pauncefote and his
colleagues on the British delegation secured the establishment of what is now known as the Hague tribunal.
When the Conference of 1899 broke up there was a general
expectation that another meeting would be held within a
few years, and periodical meetings would follow at short
intervals. This was frustrated by the war between Russia
and Japan in 1904. A proposal for the renewal of the
Conference made in that year by the United States had
no immediate result. Peace having been made in 1905
through the mediation of the same Power, Russia took
up the matter again, and the second Conference was held
in 1907; it is stated in the " Final Act " to have been first
proposed by the President of the United States, and, on
the request of the Emperor of Russia, convened by the
Queen of the Netherlands. In several ways the proceedings were better ordered than those of 1899, although
the procedure was still cumbrous; but the chance of establishing a regular period for the meetings had passed away.

At the Conference of 1907 forty-four Powers were represented, practically all the civilized States. The conventions of 1899 were reaffirmed with additions and amendments, and a new supplementary scheme for a permanent
court of justice, to which we shall return, was formulated
as being desirable (b). As to the limitation of warlike
expenditure the Conference could only declare that it

(b) Annexe to Vœu No. 1.

would be an excellent thing if the governments would take up the matter seriously.

We are not concerned here with the Conventions relating to the duties of belligerents and neutrals in time of war, nor with the causes that prevented them from being effective to any considerable extent during the war of 1914.

It is to be observed that the delegates had no authority to bind their governments; therefore each convention is formally binding (c) only on those Powers which have ratified it; moreover, some ratifications were given subject to reservations. In considering the application of any convention to a particular case it is necessary to note carefully which Powers have ratified with or without reserve, and which have abstained. Some of the conventions and declarations have, nevertheless, been acted upon by Powers which did not ratify them. Peaceable settlement of international disputes is dealt with by the Convention which stands first. The amendments of 1907 were ratified by a considerable majority in number of the States represented. Two great Powers, Great Britain and Italy, have never ratified them: but Great Britain accepted them in practice for the purpose of the North Atlantic Fisheries arbitration.

The first title of the Convention merely affirms its general object. The second is intended to encourage recourse to good offices and mediation; the proffer of either

---

(c) The Conventions as passed by the Conference, after being prepared by committees or sub-committees, were annexed to the Final Act, but assent to the Final Act did not imply assent to the particular contents of any Convention.

at any stage of a dispute is in no case to be regarded as an unfriendly act. It does not seem useful to dwell on the details, as these articles have never been called into play so far as we know.

The third title recommends the formation of international commissions of inquiry for reporting on questions of fact in difference between governments which cannot agree on them by ordinary diplomatic means (Arts. 9—14 of 1899; the additional articles of 1907 relate only to procedure). Obviously such a recommendation enables the parties to do nothing they could not do without it; moreover it is expressly declared that the report of the commission is not an award nor in any way conclusive.

Altogether these clauses belong to the class of merely optional and unsanctioned proposals which advocates of militarism have always denounced as futile. But in fact they did good practical service on the occasion of the Dogger Bank mishap in 1904; indeed it is by no means clear that if they had not been available the good offices of the French government would have been successful in averting hostility between Great Britain and Russia. The Russian fleet on its outward voyage from the Baltic to the seat of war in the East, had opened fire on the Dogger Bank fishing fleet in the night of Oct. 21 to 22, under the impression that it was in the presence of hostile torpedo boats. Diplomatic correspondence ensued, and reference to a commission of inquiry under this Convention was suggested simultaneously, it appears, at the British (*d*)

(*d*) Parl. Papers, 1905, Russia No. 2, Nos. 17, 19, 22, 28.

Foreign Office and at the Russian Court. One may conjecture that in both quarters the suggestion was inspired by
the French government, whose efforts to preserve friendly
relations were notorious at the time if not officially
recorded. The terms of reference to a mixed commission
of naval officers were substantially settled in a very short
time, and agreed on by a formal declaration of Nov. 25 (e),
after a little discussion raised by the Russian government
on a special term which charged the commission to ascer-
tain who was responsible for the acts complained of, and in
what degree any persons found answerable were to blame.
In the Russian view this went beyond the scope of the Convention, which applies only to controversies "provenant
d'une divergence d'appréciation sur des points de fait."
It seems to have really been immaterial whether it did
so or not, for the parties were free to make their own terms,
and critical historians are likewise free to say, as they
prefer, that the inquiry was held under Arts. 9 to 14 of
the Convention for the peaceable settlement of disputes
between nations, but with an agreed extension of the commissioners' authority, or that it was an inquiry by a special
commission framed on the model of those articles, though
not exactly conforming to them. The result was to con-
vince everyone except the Russian representative that the
Japanese torpedo boats were an illusion—though a more
natural one than mere landsmen would think—and the
Russian government was liable for the damage; but the
report was in such terms as to save the honour of the

(e) 1904, Treaty Series, No. 13.

Russian naval service, and was accepted by all concerned. So the way remained open to the better general understanding between the British and Russian governments which came a few years later. The wiser heads, to be sure, were determined from the first not to play into the hands of those who had most to gain by war, or, failing war, by an estrangement between Britain and Russia serious enough to prevent the British weight from being thrown into the scale of the Franco-Russian alliance in any coming European trouble. But the accident was novel, exasperating, and at first sight incapable of rational explanation. Public opinion in England was inflamed, and it was urgent to put the matter in a way of settlement at once, lest some outbreak of violent words, if not more, should render conciliation impossible. The present writer has often wondered what the chance of keeping the peace would have been if we had then lived under the democratic control of foreign policy for which some well-meaning pacifists cry aloud. He believes that if the people at large had been called on to vote in the first forty-eight hours they would have voted for instant war; he is not sure even about the House of Commons if it had been sitting. But this is not to the present purpose.

Title iv. of the Convention deals with arbitration; the provisions for procedure were simplified in 1907. Arbitration treaties may deal with existing or future disputes; they may include all manner of causes, or be limited to a specified class; they imply an undertaking to accept the award in good faith; the Powers reserve the right of making new agreements to extend the scope of compulsory arbitration as between the parties thereto (Arts. 15—19 of 1899, 37—40 of 1907). The Standing Court of Arbitration is presumed to have cognizance of cases referred to arbitration without other express provision of a tribunal. It sits and has its registry at the Hague; the Powers are bound to furnish official copies of arbitration treaties, awards, and the instruments by which awards are executed (Arts. 20—22 of 1899, 41—43 of 1907). We now come to the provisions for constituting the tribunal.

Every Power which is a party to the Convention appoints not more than four competent persons who are willing to act as arbitrators if called upon; any two or more Powers may join, if they so agree, in the nomination of one or more members, or different Powers may independently choose the same person. The nomination is for six years and renewable; casual vacancies are filled in the same manner. From the list thus made up the arbitrators have to be selected in every case referred to the standing Court. Subject to any special agreement, each party names two arbitrators, of whom only one may be a subject of its own, or (f) one of the members of the Court appointed by itself. The arbitrators choose an umpire; if they cannot agree the umpire is named by a third Power whom the parties have agreed upon for that purpose. Failing such last mentioned agreement, each party nominates a Power, and the two proceed to choose an umpire (g)

(f) This limitation was added in 1907.
(g) If those two Powers cannot agree within two months, each has to offer the names of two members of the Court not being

(Arts. 23, 24, 1899; Arts. 44, 45, 1907). The members of the tribunal, while it is sitting, have the privileges of diplomatic officers; they have the use of the buildings and staff of the Court at the Hague. It is open to Powers not parties to the Convention to avail themselves of the Court (Arts. 24—26, 1899; Arts. 45—47, 1907). In case of a critical controversy between any of the contracting Powers, it is declared to be the duty as well as the right of the rest to remind them that the Court is open (Art. 27, 1899; Art. 48, 1907). It does not appear that this article has ever been acted upon. It obviously contemplates a case in which a majority of the Great Powers would not be immediately involved in the quarrel, and could be more or less impartial counsellors. Even so, however, the duty nominally declared is a rather invidious duty which cannot be enforced in any way, and is not very likely to be performed. In 1914 the existence of the Court was brought to the notice of the Austrian and German governments by the Serbian offer to refer to it the few points of the Austrian ultimatum that were not conceded, and the offer was wholly ignored.

An administrative Board, consisting of the diplomatic representatives of the contracting Powers at the Hague, with the Foreign Minister of the Netherlands as chairman, is charged with the regulation of the permanent office there (Arts. 28, 29, 1899; Arts. 49, 50, 1907).

There follows an elaborate chapter on procedure, opera-

subjects or appointees of the parties, and the umpire is chosen from these four by lot (Art. 45 of 1907).

tive only so far as the parties to any arbitration may have left the matter open. It is conceived that most British or American lawyers would suppose the tribunal, once constituted for hearing a cause, to have inherent discretion in regulating its own proceedings—a discretion limited, of course, by the elementary rules of judicial fairness—and would expect very little to be laid down beforehand in detail. Some things, no doubt, require definition as being beyond the general control of the tribunal itself, especially when the parties are sovereign States; such are the validity of a majority decision and the incidence of costs. In others a free judicial hand would seem best. But this apparently was not the view of the draftsman, and the chapter before us reads almost as if it were addressed to people who had never heard of a court of justice. However, those who study this Convention will learn, if they did not know it before, that an arbitration cannot proceed until the terms of reference are settled and accepted by both parties. In 1907 some rather ingenious clauses (53, 54) were added, enabling the Court itself to settle the reference at the desire of the parties, or even on the request of one on certain conditions, namely (1) where the case falls within a general arbitration treaty providing for a special agreement of reference ("qui prévoit pour chaque différend un compromis"), and does not express or imply that the Court shall not be competent to settle it (but if the other party declares that it does not consider the main question within its treaty obligation the jurisdiction is excluded); (2) where the dispute arises from a claim by one Power on another for contract debts due to its subjects, and arbitration has been agreed to (unless there is some different provision for settling the terms of reference). This plan, it will be seen, is fenced about with such abundant caution that its practical utility seems to lie within very narrow bounds. It might in special circumstances assist a government desirous of a settlement, but in fear of domestic criticism and anxious to take as little responsibility as possible for the details of procedure.

The terms of reference being fixed, the Court constituted, and its seat (presumably The Hague) and the language of the proceedings determined (Arts. 32—36, 1899; 55 —61, 1907), the parties nominate agents to conduct their cases, and those agents may instruct advocates; a member of the standing panel of judges may act or appear only for the Power which appointed him a member (Art. 37, 1899; 62 of 1907). The usual procedure is by exchange of printed cases, counter-cases, and arguments, followed by oral argument before the tribunal, in public only if the Court so orders with the consent of the parties. After the close of the oral argument the Court deliberates in private, and decides, if not unanimous, by simple majority. The award must be accompanied by reasons (Arts. 39—52, 1899; 63—79, 1907). The Court may require the production of any material documents (Arts. 43, 44, 1899; 68—69, 1907). An award may be reviewed by the Court only under power expressly reserved to the parties in the agreement of reference to call for revision on the discovery of new material facts (Art. 55, 1899; 83, 1907). Each party bears its own costs and half the expenses of the Court (Art. 57, 1899; 85, 1907).

In 1907 provision was made for the disposal of causes
admitting of summary procedure by two arbitrators and
an umpire without hearing oral argument (Arts. 86—90).
It is possible to read these clauses as intended to establish
a presumption in favour of the summary method; the
correctness or otherwise of such a reading does not appear
material, for it is hardly conceivable that two Powers
should go to arbitration without expressing their inten-
tions as to the formation of the tribunal and its procedure
in their agreement of reference. There does not appear
to have been in fact any example of this summary process,
but it would save both time and expense in cases not
involving any dispute of principle. If it be said that
the parties are masters of the procedure in any case where
they choose to specify it beforehand, and can make it as
summary as they will without the help of the Court, we
have to answer to this, as to other like objections, that
the provision of a standing form which can be adopted
at pleasure is a well-tried instrument for saving time and
trouble in many kinds of affairs, and is therefore not to
be dismissed as superfluous.

Before the war there was much academic discussion of
the question whether the Hague tribunal is a real court
of justice. As the conclusion depends on every writer's
taste in definitions, I am humbly of opinion that this is
not a very profitable argument. Any man may say, if
he likes, that there can be no proper court without compulsory jurisdiction and executive power; but in that case
he may be driven to deny that the King's Court in
England was a proper court much before the thirteenth

century, in which he cannot expect many English lawyers
or historians to agree with him. If he extends his view
to Iceland his troubles will thicken, for he will find there,
about the time of the Norman Conquest, regularly held
courts with an elaborate procedure, whose decisions are
for the most part obeyed, and yet having no means whatever of executing them, and no sanction other than public
opinion (*h*).

It must be admitted, certainly, that the Peace Conferences did not establish a permanent court. What they
did provide was the framework of a tribunal and a method
of constituting it from time to time as and when required.
Being so constituted, the tribunal dealing with each case
is a judicial body and bound to act judicially. The
machinery has been put in action several times, and in
one case of great importance, that of the Newfoundland
fisheries; it has worked without any serious hitch, and
carefully considered awards have been made after full
argument, accepted and acted upon. Defects may be
found in any court of justice, and no one maintains that
the Hague tribunal is a perfect court. To deny that it
is a court of justice at all, or that it has done some fairly
effectual justice, appears to me to be a feat of rather high
dialectical courage.

One feature of the Hague tribunal is that the acting
judges on each occasion are chosen directly or indirectly
by the parties. As to this it may be relevant to observe
that well within living memory there were four judges of

(*h*) Cp. the present writer's Notes B and C to Maine's Ancient
Law.

first instance, the Master of the Rolls and three Vice-Chancellors, in the English Court of Chancery, and it was in the choice of the party commencing a suit by which of them the case should be heard. That choice was determined by various reasons according to the nature of the case. Practitioners who sought an authoritative decision on a question of law set down their causes before that great lawyer Sir George Jessel, Master of the Rolls. There were also those who desired, under the forms of litigation, to secure the aid and direction of the Court in administering estates and settling family affairs for the next generation. They knew where to find a Vice-Chancellor whose benevolent discretion, if confronted with a doubt of the Court's competence, would make a liberal application of the maxim *Boni iudicis est ampliare iurisdictionem* to carry out the intention of the parties. It did not occur to any one to think that arrangements of this kind impaired the judicial character or authority of the Court of Chancery.

We have seen that the arbitration Court established by the Hague Peace Conferences is called into active existence only by the reference to arbitration of a specific dispute between two Powers, and the selection of judges to form a tribunal for the occasion in the prescribed manner. In 1907 a considerable number of the delegates wished, in addition to this, to set up a constant judicial court, which should hold regular sittings, and whose judges should be told off for duty by its own rules and not by the choice of the parties. This plan was embodied in a draft Convention annexed to the Final Act, and recommended for adoption; but in consequence of the claim made on behalf of several minor Powers to an absolutely equal standing in the appointment of judges, to which the delegates of the greater Powers naturally did not agree, the matter did not go farther (i). The draft was made acceptable as far as it went only by the total omission of this contentious topic. The opposing delegates, headed by the eloquent and persistent Brazilian, Ruy Barbosa (k), appear to have confused the principles of juridical and political equality. All nations have equal rights as between themselves, like citizens in one State. It does not follow that all must have equal voices and votes in all matters of common interest. One would like to ask M. Ruy Barbosa whether it is, or he thinks it ought to be, the law of Brazil that at a company meeting every shareholder has one and only one vote without regard to the number of shares he holds. But another and perhaps even deeper fallacy is involved in the claim of one judge and no more for every State. The object is not representation of the contracting Powers as such either equally or in proportion to their importance; it is to form the best and most impartial court that can be devised. A court of justice is not a political senate, and the less it resembles one in substance or in form the better. The only reason for having the judges nominated by the governments of

(i) Cp. Pearce Higgins, The Hague Peace Conferences, pp. 509—517.

(k) He professed to take his stand on " principes juridiques d'un ordre capital " (2me Conf. ii., 696); it is not really a legal question at all.

the constituent States was that no other nominators were at hand (*l*); and the true reason for giving a greater share to the greater Powers appears to be that their rulers are more likely to command or attract the services of the persons best qualified for membership of the proposed court. It seems a tenable view that the system of "one State, one judge" might be made tolerable by requiring the consent of some expert standing committee to the nominations; otherwise under that system there would really be no security for the persons appointed being in every case competent or even honestly chosen for their supposed competence. But we shall have to return to this subject, which is still at large, in commenting on the fundamental articles of the League of Nations.

In other respects the draft Convention is a carefully framed instrument, and will no doubt be found useful when the League of Nations is ready to take up the business of establishing a court.

Inasmuch as the text is easily accessible, and it is most unlikely that it will ever take effect according to the letter, it will suffice for our purpose to give only a summary account of its contents. The establishment of the proposed new court was expressly stated to be without prejudice to the functions of the tribunal provided by the Conference of 1899 ("sans porter atteinte à la cour permanente

(*l*) Why not the highest judicial authorities in each country? Because the judicial establishments of different nations are so differently constituted that no uniform system would be possible. There are even civilized European States that have, or quite lately had, no professional judges at all. Governments, on the other hand, can always obtain expert advice officially or semi-officially.

d'arbitrage "). We have already explained that its number and composition, and the mode of appointment, were left at large, but it was laid down (Art. 2) that the members must be of the highest character, and either qualified for superior judicial office (" la haute magistrature ") in their own countries, or jurists of well-known competence in international law. They were, moreover, to be selected so far as might be from the members of the existing tribunal. They were to hold office for twelve years and be re-eligible (Art. 3). A special commission (" délégation ") of three judges, with the like number to replace them at need, was to be named every year by the court itself; this commission was to convene the court once a year unless it appeared that there was no business for it (Art. 14). Apparently the ordinary acting court was to consist of the delegation, with two other judges nominated by the parties in each case as assessors (Arts. 6, 20); but on this point the draft is neither clear nor well arranged, and one cannot help suspecting that several clauses were struck out at the last moment to avoid disagreement. Indeed it is obvious that nothing could be said about sittings of the full court or divisions thereof so long as the number of its members remained unsettled.

The new judicial office was to carry a salary of 6,000 Dutch gulden (approximately 500*l*. sterling), and a fee of 100 gulden a day (say eight guineas) for the judicial work actually done (Art. 9). It is needless to refer particularly to the provisions for the presidency of the Court, exclusion of judges representing interested parties, regulation of procedure and other matters of detail.

The scheme was of American origin, and brought' forward by the United States delegates in conjunction with those of Great Britain and Germany. So long as there was no talk of compulsory jurisdiction there was nothing against it from the point of view of German policy; rather it may have seemed useful for Germany to appear on the progressive side for once. The Prussian General Staff, having its own doctrine of overriding military necessity in reserve, and making no secret of it (*m*), attached very little importance to anything that a Hague Conference might formulate at this or any other time; and German academic opinion was in favour of the more solemn judicial form as against the elastic and unpretentious method of special arbitration agreements. One or two learned writers even belittled arbitration much as indiscreet advocates of arbitration and panegyrists of the Hague tribunal had belittled the resources of ordinary diplomacy. It is a curious fact that the only express dissent came from the Swiss government.

Early in 1914 the United States resumed the subject in a very full memorandum, the work of Dr. James Brown Scott, addressed to the Foreign Minister of the Netherlands government. It was there proposed that a permanent court should be established by those Powers which had shown their approval of such an institution—prac-

(*m*) The tractate "Kriegsbrauch im Landkriege," now notorious, was one of a long series of technical military publications and almost escaped the attention of civilian publicists at the time. It is in vol. 6 of "Kriegsgeschichtliche Einzelschriften." Cp. Westlake, Collated Papers (1914), pp. 243—280.

tically all the Great Powers and the Netherlands—with jurisdiction as between those Powers only.

This memorandum was intended to be communicated to the other Powers whose agreement was thought probable, as well as to the Dutch Foreign Office. It does not appear what steps had been taken in this direction before the outbreak of war in Europe made any further action impossible.

In the result, the judicial institution created by the first Peace Conference continued to stand alone, improved by certain amendments. The treaties of wider scope initiated by the United States, of which we have already spoken (p. 38, above), are wholly independent of the Hague court, and distinct from all ordinary types of arbitral proceedings and reference to arbitration.

CHAPTER IV.

THE LEAGUE IN SIGHT.

References.

A. Lawrence Lowell, A League to enforce Peace. World Peace Foundation, Boston, Mass., 1915. Enforced Peace: proceedings of the first annual national assemblage of the League to enforce Peace, Washington, May 26th—27th, 1916. New York, 1916.

Theodore Marburg, League of Nations: a chapter in the history of the movement. New York, 1917.

Report of a conference of the legal profession. London : League of Nations Society, 1917.

Leonard S. Woolf (ed.), The framework of a lasting peace. London, 1917. Seven schemes are printed in full (list at p. 59).

International Government: two reports prepared for the Fabian Research Department. London [1916].

Henry Noel Brailsford, A League of Nations. London, 1917.

Draft Convention for League of Nations, by group of American jurists and publicists. Description and comment by Theodore Marburg. New York, 1918. [Mr. Marburg's part, with some verbal changes, is reprinted in the Journal of Comparative Legislation, April, 1918.]

A scheme for the World League. Speech delivered by the late Lord Parker in the House of Lords on March 19th, 1918. (League of Nations Union pamphlet, Series 2, No. 16.)

Gen. J. C. Smuts, The League of Nations: a practical suggestion. London, 1918.

Proceedings of the conference of delegates of allied societies for a League of Nations, London, March 11th—13th, 1919. League of Nations Union.

The Peace Conference and after. Introduction by Viscount Gray of Fallodon. Reprint from The Round Table, December, 1918. London: Macmillan & Co., 1919.

———

THE relations between civilized nations in the matter of doing justice to one another and settling disputes, as they appeared to stand after the second Peace Conference and before the war of 1914, may be summed up as follows. When we say before the war, we exclude the " Bryan treaties " for reference to a joint commission of " non-justiciable" disputes without any exception; these, as we have seen, were concluded only from the latter part of 1914 onwards.

There was no jurisdiction to hear and determine disputes between sovereign States except by consent given either in a standing Convention of the parties, or in a special agreement to refer the case to arbitral decision. But there was a method of appointing an arbitral tribunal by selection from a standing list of competent persons, and there was the official establishment of a court with a local habitation and records at The Hague. Most Powers were bound by a number of conventions of similar type to refer to the tribunal so provided all such disputes as did not affect their independence, honour, or vital interests. A network of these arbitration agreements was enfolding the community of nations, and it looked almost as if the substance of a practically universal treaty for the settlement at any rate of "justiciable" disputes would be attained without the formalities of a general congress. It seemed that on the whole sovereign States were willing to do as well as to expect justice. That was the opinion of so practical a man of affairs as Mr. Elihu Root in the year following the second Peace Conference.

"For the great mass of mankind laws established by civil society are enforced directly by the power of public opinion, having, as the sanction for its judgments, the denial of nearly everything for which men strive in life.

"The rules of international law are enforced by the same kind of sanction, less certain and peremptory, but continually increasing in effectiveness of control. . . . .

"The real sanction which enforces those rules is the injury which inevitably follows nonconformity to public opinion" (a).

Some years later Mr. Root was forced to allow that, in common with many other well-informed persons, he had been disappointed. "If the law of nations is to be binding," he said near the end of the year 1915, "if the decisions of tribunals charged with the application of that law to international controversies are to be respected, there must be a change in theory, and violations of the law of such a character as to threaten the peace and order of the community of nations must be deemed to be a violation of the right of every civilized nation to have the law maintained and a legal injury to every nation." The need for establishing new and effectual sanctions by common accord could not be better stated. The present writer had said, also about 1908, that for the prevention of wars of ambition "only one remedy would be quite effectual, namely that a coalition of Powers of superior collective strength should be prepared to enforce the principles which now stand unanimously acknowledged by the second Peace Conference of the Hague" (b).

Meanwhile certain publicists, especially Prof. Schücking (c), had gone so far as to maintain that the Hague tribunal, and the permanent machinery for constituting it,

(a) Presidential address to the American Society of International Law, 1908, in "Addresses on International Subjects," Cambridge, Mass., 1916.

(b) Cambridge Modern History, xii., 719.

(c) See at head of Chapter III., above.

together with the body of Conventions framed by the Peace
Conferences, amounted to the formation of a quasi-federal
union embracing the signatory States. This can be regarded, in my humble opinion, only as the speculative
thesis of an adventurous minority. So far as I know it
has not been adopted by any English-speaking writer.
In any' case there is no continuity between the concert,
agreement, or whatever it should be called, expressed in
the proceedings of the Hague Conferences, and the new
system of the League of Nations, and therefore no practical question arises. Nor does it seem useful to consider
whether in strict theory it is possible to recognize any
federal or approximately federal character in agreements
which wholly omit to provide any real common authority
for · either judicial, legislative, or executive purposes.
Here it must be remembered that the Hague tribunal
derives its authority only from the agreement of the
parties in each case. The forms put at their disposal by
the Conventions are indeed common forms, but they are
binding only so far as adopted for the occasion, and they
can be and on some occasions have been modified (*d*).

(*d*) From the point of view of form or rather formlessness, the
substantive rules of the community of nations, as they existed
before the war of 1914, were singularly like those of a certain
professional club of learned persons in London as reported and
collected by a very diligent secretary. He wrote of them as
follows: " It is practically impossible to give the rules in full.
Rules are to be found in written form scattered about the records
of the club; but of these several have been modified by usage
and some have fallen into disuse. Other rules are founded on
tradition and have never been formally put into writing." The
resemblance is the more curious because that club, having been

Even before 1914 the purely voluntary scheme of the
Hague tribunal was not generally accepted as final, and
many plans for a more effectual agreement among civilized
Powers were put forward by various writers down to the
time when the Peace Conference of Paris took the matter
seriously in hand. Some of these plans, aiming at a
complete federal constitution with a super-national government, were altogether extravagant; one or two of their
authors offered a complete new code of international law
ready made. Others of more moderate ambition were
overweighted by an excess of premature detail; nevertheless the ventilation of the subject was useful and many
of the suggestions profitable. The definite beginning of
a practical movement towards a league of nations was
the foundation of the American League to enforce Peace,
which took place at a meeting held at Philadelphia on
June 17, 1915. If any men are to be specially named
as the prime movers, they are Mr. William H. Taft, formerly President of the United States, who had already
indicated the main points in an address delivered in May,
1915, to the American society for judicial settlement of
international disputes, founded in 1910, and Mr. Theodore
Marburg, formerly United States Minister in Belgium,
whom Mr. Taft has himself singled out (e). With excellent good sense and discretion, Mr. Taft and his com-

founded in 1815, is exactly coeval with the Congress of Vienna.
Comparison of small things with great is not necessarily frivolous;
at times it may even be profitable.

(e) In his foreword to Mr. Marburg's "League of Nations,"
New York, 1917.

panions laid down the principles of their league in four articles only, without anticipating matters of detail. Those articles run as follows:—

It is desirable for the United States to join in a league of nations binding the signatories to the following:—

1. All justiciable questions arising between the signatory Powers, not settled by negotiation, shall, subject to the limitations of treaties, be submitted to a judicial tribunal for hearing and judgment, both upon the merits and upon any issue as to its jurisdiction of the question.

2. All other questions arising between the signatories and not settled by negotiation shall be submitted to a Council of Conciliation for hearing, consideration, and recommendation.

3. The signatory Powers shall jointly use forthwith both their economic and military forces against any one of their number that goes to war, or commits acts of hostility, against another of the signatories before any question arising shall be submitted as provided in the foregoing.

[The following interpretation of this article was authorized by the Executive Committee:—The signatory Powers shall jointly employ diplomatic and economic pressure against any of their number that threatens war against a fellow signatory without having first submitted its dispute for international inquiry, conciliation, arbitration, or judicial hearing, and awaited a conclusion, or without having in good faith offered so to submit it. They shall

follow this forthwith by the joint use of their military
forces against that nation if it actually goes to war, or
commits acts of hostility against another of the signatories
before any question arising shall be dealt with as provided in the foregoing.]

    4. Conferences between the signatory Powers shall
    be held from time to time to formulate and codify
    rules of international law, which, unless some signa-
    tory shall signify its dissent within a stated period,
    shall thereafter govern in the decisions of the judicial
    tribunal mentioned in Article 1.

Thus, thanks to the efforts of publicists on both sides
of the Atlantic, working in small groups whose competence and perseverance made up for their lack of
numbers, the League of Nations was fairly before the
public in the second year of the great war not as an
academic fancy, but as a serious political ideal. Accordingly militarist politicians and journalists (for it cannot
be concealed that militarism is to be found among the
Western Allies) no longer treated it as negligible, but
began to denounce it as a mischievous delusion and no
better than a branch of pacifist propaganda. Now it is
quite true that some pacifists both in belligerent and in
neutral countries dreamt of a league after their own
fashion which would disclaim coercive power and trust
to organizing moral opinion. Incredible as it may seem
that in 1916, 1917, and 1918 these people still believed
that war could be done away with by shouting "no more
war" and framing pious resolutions, it is a fact we have
witnessed. Holland was the chief centre of their more

innocent activities, and in a lesser degree the Scandinavian countries; in Switzerland others were established which, including as they did such methods as wilful falsification of recent diplomatic history, were less innocent. Some allowance must be made for the invincible incapacity of sane judgment which may lead to an honestly held though enormously foolish opinion that all war is equally criminal, all governments equally fraudulent, and all disputes between nations equally frivolous. But I have never been able to understand the special perversity whereby British followers of this persuasion almost always argue (not scrupling, as above hinted, to tamper with the evidence) that, although every one concerned in making war must be desperately wicked, their own countrymen are rather worse than others. As we are not undertaking a pathological study of civic dementia, no more shall be said of these follies. We shall see that the actual founders of the League of Nations fully recognize the need of visible power to enforce its principles, though we may regret that they did not see their way to make their provision for such an emergency more explicit.

Following the American lead, associations with like aims were formed in France (Association française pour une société des nations), England (League of Nations Society and League of Free Nations Association) (f), and Italy. As regards the two English societies, the former inclined to doctrines of cosmopolitan pacifism as formu-

---

(f) To be distinguished from a society of like name at New York having a much more elaborate and mainly economic platform.

lated before the war, while the latter was founded on the conviction that the victory of the Western Allies must be frankly accepted as the necessary condition of any real security for peace; in November, 1918, the two bodies were amalgamated by the name of the League of Nations Union, and it would be useless for any purpose of the present work to dwell on their original differences. Since the beginning of 1919 the American, British, French and other societies have been working in concert, and in March of that year a conference of delegates of allied societies was held in London. It included, besides strong American, British, and French delegations, representatives from Greece, China, the South Slavonic Kingdom, and Rumania (g).

During the last two years of the war there was a steady convergence of responsible opinion agreeing in general terms on the necessity of providing some definite sanction for the observance of international law, and security against aggressive wars, by common agreement among civilized nations. The moral weight of opinion having proved insufficient for want of immediate coercive power, it remained to devise means whereby any wilful breaker of the peace would be confronted with the united strength of an overwhelming majority.

Early in 1917 (Jan. 10) the Western allied Powers expressed to the President of the United States "their whole-hearted agreement with the proposal to create a League of Nations which shall assure peace and justice throughout

(g) See Note D at end of this chapter for a list down to 1919.

the world," and recognized the benefit to be expected
" from the institution of international arrangements designed to prevent violent conflicts between nations, and
so framed as to provide the sanctions necessary to their
enforcement, lest an illusory security should serve merely
to facilitate fresh acts of aggression."

On March 19, 1918, the late Lord Parker, speaking in
the House of Lords on a motion made by Lord Parmoor,
stated carefully and at some length what he thought the
essential points of a practical agreement. Evidently his
object was to smooth the way for action by postponing or
evading the more troublesome questions of detail. In
particular he suggested that the constituent nations might
bind themselves to take steps for the peaceable settlement
of disputes before resorting to arms, without being bound
as to the method of settlement. It would be open to them
to use the Hague tribunal or proceed in any other manner
agreed upon either by standing treaties or on the special
occasion. The Covenant as now accepted goes distinctly
beyond Lord Parker's proposal, but his speech did excellent
service in preparing and enlightening public opinion, and
above all in making it plain that the matter was to be
taken seriously.

Most unfortunately Lord Parker was disabled from con-
tinuing his work by illness which proved fatal. He died
on the 6th of July, to the grievous loss of his country, his
profession, and his friends. On June 26, 1918, Lord
Curzon said on behalf of the government in the course of
the resumed debate:—" We want to do something to prevent wars, or, if that is too Utopian an aspiration, to limit

their scope and to diminish their horrors in future. For this purpose a general concurrence of nations is necessary, and if it is to be effective it ought ultimately to include all the important States of the world. . . . We must try to get some alliance, or confederation, or conference to which these States shall belong, and no State in which shall be at liberty to go to war without reference or [? to] arbitration, or to a conference of the League, in the first place. Then if a State breaks the contract it will become, *ipso facto*, at war with the other States in the League, and they will support each other, without any need for an international police, in punishing or in repairing the breach of contract. Some of them may do it by economic pressure. This may apply perhaps to the smaller States. The larger and more powerful States may do it by the direct use of naval and military force. In this way we may not indeed abolish war, but we can render it a good deal more difficult in the future. These are the only safe and practicable lines at present, and the lines upon which the government are disposed to proceed."

It will be observed that the automatic nature of the sanction, a point of the utmost importance in the present writer's judgment, is here made conspicuous.

One of Lord Parker's points was that a league of nations might very well get to work without waiting to solve the problems arising from the determination to create a new court of international justice. What is essential to the covenant of peace is that the contracting Powers should undertake not to go to war without obtaining or endeavouring in good faith to obtain some kind of peaceable settle-

ment or award, not that the resort should in every case be
to the same tribunal, nor even that it should be in judicial
form. The immediate purpose will be served alike whether
they go before a tribunal formed under the Hague Conventions, or set up a court or board of arbitrators by
special agreement, or refer the whole matter to the titular
head of some friendly State, who will of course fortify
himself with expert advice of the best. This is quite
consistent with holding that it is desirable to establish a
permanent court whose continuity will enable it to establish a judicial tradition and to speak with authority extending beyond the settlement of particular disputes.

In the latter part of 1918, when the last desperate offen-
sive of the German armies had definitely failed, it was
clear that the speculative stage of the great problem was
already past. The only question was whether the constitution of the League of Nations should be considered
by the delegates of the Allies as part of the terms of peace,
or postponed till after the conclusion of the treaty. European opinion was divided; the government of the United
States was strongly in favour of keeping the League of
Nations in the front and making adherence to its principles
one of the conditions of the peace; and this view prevailed
when the armistice of November made a prompt decision
urgent. In December Gen. Smuts wrote a pamphlet
which, as it was the latest, was the most effective contribution made by individual enterprise. He had, to be
sure, the advantage of knowing a great deal more about
the joint actions and discussions already undertaken by
the Allies than any previous writer on the subject. What-

ever was the precise amount of that advantage, his antici-
pation came remarkably near to the result attained a few
months later by a committee in whose work he is understood to have had a leading part. Gen. Smuts's "practical
suggestion" differed from most other proposals both in
what it omitted or minimized and what it insisted upon.
Negatively, it left the establishment of a judicial tribunal
in a rather vague background. Positively, it emphasized
the continuous duty of the League to exercise control over
international property (not a new thing in itself, for it
has been done for many years by mixed commissions),
and to supervise the administration of common undertakings, including the government of populations released
from the dominion of enemy Powers, but not ripe for
autonomy.

The only definite organs of the League of Nations contemplated by Gen. Smuts's pamphlet were a general conference or congress, assembled on the footing of equality
between all constituent States, and an executive council in
which permanent representation would give the Great
Powers a small majority. Courts of arbitration and conciliation were indeed mentioned, but no details were given;
Gen. Smuts indeed seems to regard it as of small importance, for the present at any rate, whether they should be
permanent or formed, as committees of the larger body
or otherwise, only as the special occasion may require.
In fact the arrangement he suggested resembles that of
the Hague tribunal, the difference being that the panel
of possible judges is framed by the council of the League.
Mediation, where desirable, should be exercised by the

council itself. Any member of the League making war on another without submission of the dispute for award or report, or, after award or report, against a member complying therewith, should, in Gen. Smuts's own words, " become *ipso facto* at war with all the other members of the League, great and small alike, which will sever all relations of trade and finance with the law-breaker, and prohibit all intercourse with its subjects, and also prevent as far as possible all commercial and financial intercourse between the subjects of the law-breaker and those of any other State, whether a member of the League or not. No declaration of war should be necessary, as the state of war arises automatically on the law-breaker proceeding to hostilities, and the boycott follows automatically from the obligation of the League without further resolutions or formalities on the part of the League." We have already called attention to this point of automatic execution as being of special importance; an offender should not have the chance of gaining time for intrigue, or seizing a vital strategic position while the Powers are deliberating.

Meanwhile a Convention of a more elaborate type had been drafted by a group of American publicists (not an official committee of the League to enforce Peace) earlier in 1918; it is the latest specimen of this type and perhaps the best. An account of it was contributed by Mr. Theodore Marburg to the Journal of Comparative Legislation. Its leading character is much more precise definition of executive and judicial functions.

Before proceeding to consider the constitution and functions of the League of Nations as laid down in outline

by the Peace Conference of 1919, it may be useful to call
attention to the number and variety of international conventions already in force for the regulation of communications and transport, administration of treaty provisions,
collection of statistics and intelligence in matters of commerce and industry, and similar cosmopolitan purposes.
There has been much alarm about the interference with
the sovereignty of independent States which it is alleged
that the League of Nations will entail. Few if any of
the objectors have noticed that the parties to the League
have already limited their freedom of action in many
directions by these existing conventions. They can indeed
release themselves by withdrawal, but only with notice
and in due form; and in the more important cases the consequences of withdrawing from the joint business would
be so inconvenient that reversion to the former state of
isolation cannot be regarded as a practical contingency.
Mr. L. S. Woolf has pointed out in his very useful reports
made for the Fabian Society (p. 103) that by one class
of these conventions provision is made " for the creation of
some permanent deliberative or legislative international
body, and also for an administrative body working under
the direction of the former "; such is the model of the
telegraphic unions and the postal and the metric union.
" The Institute of Agriculture has a very elaborate constitution, with two deliberative bodies, the General Assembly and the Permanent Committee, and a permanent
bureau."

The following statement is taken from the *Round Table*,
March, 1919 (p. 235):—" There existed before the war the

Universal Postal Union, with its permanent bureau; the International and Radio-Telegraphic Bureau; the International Railway Bureau; the Danube and Suez Canal Commissions; the International Office of Public Health at Paris, and the four International Sanitary Councils at Constantinople, Alexandria, Teheran and Tangier; various monetary and metric unions between States; the Union for the Publication of Customs Tariffs, with its permanent bureau; the permanent Sugar Commission; the International Institute of Agriculture; the International Union for the Protection of Industrial Property; the International Bureau at Zanzibar for the repression of the Slave Traffic, and certain other bodies like the International Statistical Institute."

The best known and in some ways the most typical of these cosmopolitan bodies is the Postal Union, dating from 1875. Its fundamental instruments are the Convention and a scheme of rules (Règlement); it is governed by a congress meeting nominally every five years, with power to amend both the Convention and the rules by a majority, subject to ratification; a conference of delegates of administrations (which in practice has met only once, being found unnecessary); and a permanent office at Berne. Interim amendments can be made by the national administrators, for which in some matters unanimity is required, in others a two-thirds majority, and in details of interpretation and the like a bare majority suffices: all this being done by correspondence through the central office. In practice ratification is not refused, even by governments which actively opposed the change, to amendments passed

by the required majority.   Colonies and dependencies have
separate representation and votes.   Apart from merely
verbal distinctions, it cannot be denied that every sovereign
State belonging to the Postal Union has willingly re-
nounced its sovereign right of independent action as to
foreign postal rates (*h*), and all that is implied in the
regulation of international postal traffic.   I am not aware
that any protest has come even from the most ardent
national patriots in any one of these States; and it certainly would need great courage to maintain that the
civilized world has not gained advantages amply worth the
price for this and similar institutions.   In this case no
friction has occurred in forty years' working, and little
difficulty seems to be found in making suitable exceptions
and variations for peculiar local circumstances (*i*).   We
need not dwell on the regulation of telegraphy and, on the
Continent of Europe, of railway transport; the rather that
the regulation of air traffic by international agreement is
now seen, even by the most casual observer, to be a matter
not of convenience but of the first necessity.

In contrast to the administrative unions we have a different type in the Institute of Agriculture established at
Rome, which for the present at any rate is chiefly concerned with research and information conducted under the
guidance of standing or special committees.   It includes
fifty-five States; the work of the permanent committee

(*h*) They can be modified only within the maximum prescribed
by the Union. Postage between Great Britain and the United
States was lowered from $2\frac{1}{2}d.$ to $1d.$ before the war, and raised
to $1\frac{1}{2}d.$ during the war. It could not be increased to $3d.$ without
the statutable general consent.

(*i*) Woolf, International Government, 120—129.

was not interrupted by the war of 1914 (*k*). An international maritime committee founded by private enterprise in 1898 has already done much for the uniformity of sea law (*l*).

Ultimately all international bureaux and commissions, the consent of the contracting parties being first obtained as to those already formed under general treaties, are intended to come under the direction of the League (Covenant, Art. 25). Joint action by delegates of several nations in this or that field of peaceful business does not, certainly, throw much light on the causes of war nor on the most likely means of preventing war in the future. But these various activities do show that when the importance of some common object is once admitted the practical difficulties of co-operation are far less than they would appear at first sight, and that even schemes of distributing work and control which look pretty complicated on paper do not in fact give any serious trouble. The transfer of general direction to the League of Nations will supply the facilities for co-ordination and mutual information which alone were wanting to combine these undertakings into a great international system.

NOTE D (*m*).

WORLD LEAGUE OF NATIONS MOVEMENT: LIST OF ANALOGOUS SOCIETIES.

Australia.—International Peace Society (Adelaide Branch), Wittunga Blackwood.

(*k*) *Op. cit.*, 158—164.   (*l*) *Ib.*, 171—180.
(*m*) From the League of Nations Journal, August, 1919, p. 315. The League's periodical is now enlarged as " The Covenant."

Austria.—Verband Liga für einen Völkerbund, Vienna I, Burg-
ring 9.

China.—The League of Nations Section, Association for the Study
of International Affairs, Peking, China.

The Chinese League of Nations Union, Peking, China.

France.—Ligue pour une Société des Nations, 5, Cité Cardinal
Lemoine, Paris.

Association Française pour une Société des Nations, 254,
Boulevard St. Germain, Paris.

Germany.—Deutsche Liga für Völkerbund, Berlin, Unter den
Linden 78.

Great Britain.—League of Nations Union, 22, Buckingham Gate,
London, S.W.1.

International Arbitration League, 39, Victoria Street, London,
S.W.1.

League to Abolish War, 29, Grosvenor Park, London, S.E.5.

Greece.—Ligue Hellénique pour la Société des Nations, 11, Rue
Nikis, Athens.

Holland.—The Nederlandsche Anti-Oorlog Raad, Prinsesgracht
19, The Hague.

Ireland.—The Irish "League of Nations" Society, 65, Middle
Abbey Street, Dublin.

Italy.—Liga Universelle Societe delle Libre Nazioni [*sic*], Corso
Vittorio Emanuele 8, Milan, Italy.

Japan.—The International Japan Association, 10, Onote
Sarugaku-cho, Kando, Tokio.

Norway.—Den Norske Forening for Nationernes Liga, Kristiana.

Poland.—Société Polonaise des Amis de la Ligue des Nations,
Warsaw, Poland.

S. Africa.—Peace and Arbitration Society, P.O. Box 575, Cape
Town.

Peace and Arbitration Society, P.O. Box 2317, Johannesburg.

Spain.—Union Democrática Española, Prado 11, Madrid, Spain.

Sweden.—The Swedish League of Nations Society, Stockholm,
Sweden.

Switzerland.—The Swiss League of Nations Society, Lerchenweg,
33, Berne.

United States.—The League to Enforce Peace, Bush Buildings,
130, West 42nd Street, New York City, U.S.A.

The League of Nations Union, 70, Fifth Avenue, New York, U.S.A.

The World Peace Foundation, 40, Mount Vernon Street, Boston, Mass.

The American Liberty League, Randolph, Wis., U.S.A.

The Carnegie Endowment for International Peace, 2, Jackson Place, Washington, D.C., U.S.A.

The American Rights League, 2, West 45th Street, New York City.

The Church Peace Union, 70, Fifth Avenue, New York City, U.S.A.

World Alliance for Promoting International Friendship through the Churches, 105, East 22nd Street, New York City, U.S.A.

World Court League, Incorporated Educational Buildings, Fifth Avenue, 13th Street, New York City.

Book II.—THE LEAGUE IN BEING.

CHAPTER V.

THE CONSTITUTION OF THE LEAGUE.

References.

Draft Agreement for a League of Nations, presented to the plenary inter-allied Conference of February 14, 1919. Parliamentary Papers, 1919, Cmd. 2.

The Covenant of the League of Nations, with a Commentary thereon. Parliamentary Papers, 1919, Cmd. 151. Text, pp. 3—11; Commentary, pp. 12—19.

[Both the draft and the final text, with the commentary, are set out in full in the Appendix below.]

Treaty of Peace between the allied and associated Powers and Germany signed at Versailles, June 28, 1919. Parliamentary Papers, 1919, Cmd. 153.

The League of Nations (La Société des Nations, Der Völkerbund), a weekly review. Ferd. Wyss, Berne. Documents, speeches, etc. in the original texts.

The Covenanter: Letters on the Covenant of the League of Nations, by William Howard Taft, George W. Wickersham, A. Lawrence Lowell, Henry W. Taft. Boston, Mass. World Peace Foundation, 1919.

The League of Nations: the principle and the practice. Edited by Stephen Pierce Duggan. Boston, Mass. 1919. [Includes chapters by Prof. J. B. Moore and President Lowell.]

AT the beginning of the war of 1914 men commonly thought it would be like other modern wars, only on a larger scale. It would be short; all European wars had been so since the downfall of Napoleon, and the confidence of military experts was not shaken by the length of the American Civil War, which the Prussian General Staff

regarded as an amateurish and uninstructive affair. (Lord
Kitchener's forecast of three years did not carry general
conviction when it was made, least of all to the cocksure
experts of the press.) It would be conducted in due form;
the Germans would be severe and punctilious, giving themselves the benefit of the doubt in doubtful cases, and
showing no mercy to irregular combatants, but in the
main observing the rules of civilized warfare which they
had themselves taken an active part in defining. It would
end in the regular fashion with a congress in which all
the belligerent and some important neutral Powers would
be effectively represented, and the result would be a treaty
of general settlement with a good deal of compromise on
minor points. Defeat of Germany and her allies would
probably break up the Austro-Hungarian Empire, and
might well be the ruin of the Hohenzollern dynasty too,
but these consequences would not be immediate. Active
alliance with the free nations of western Europe would be
a potent influence for constitutional reform in Russia;
the Tsar's promises nearly ten years old could no longer
be evaded; but nothing short of a great military disaster
was likely to bring about a revolution. In the event
every one of these expectations was signally falsified.
After the failure of the last desperate German attack
in 1918 the whole fabric of the Central European mon-
archies collapsed, and neither a Habsburg nor a Hohenzollern ruler was left for the victorious Allies to make peace
with. The ambitions of the new States that were emerg-
ing from the ruins had to be moderated and, so far as
possible, reconciled. Reparation on a great scale had to

be undertaken, and this involved far-reaching economic plans and constructive work such as could be executed only by the closest co-operation; insomuch that, if no one had thought of a League of Nations before, it would none the less have been needful, about the end of 1918, to invent something of the kind.

The only doubt in matter of principle was as to the time at which and the order in which things were to be done. Simultaneous proceeding with the treaty of peace and with the League was favoured by one school of opinion, and deprecated as unpractical by another. The objections of the latter would have been unanswerable if there had been no way between elaborating a constitution for the League of Nations in all its details and postponing the whole matter to a season of greater leisure. But the answer was that it was quite possible to lay down the general plan of an international covenant with sufficient certainty and in a moderate compass, or rather, as one may now say in this age of steel and concrete, set up the framework of the building. Gen. Smuts indeed gave actual proof that it could be done. Moreover, the policy of leisured elaboration involved no small risk that after the immediate pressure of the peace settlement was removed the standing argument "Why can't you let it alone?", an argument very dear to old-fashioned diplomacy, would re-assert itself and prevail. The decision was in favour of immediate action; we cannot expect to know in our time the course of the debates by which it was reached, or whether the consent of all parties was alike willing. So it was that in February, 1919, the delegates of fourteen States pre-

sented the draft of an agreement for a league of nations
to the plenary conference of the Allies in Paris. This draft
was submitted to further revision, in the course of which
neutral governments were also consulted. " In its revised
form it was unanimously accepted by the representatives
of the Allied and Associated Powers in Plenary Conference at Paris on April 28, 1919 " (a). It is an integral
section, not being an annex but standing first, in the treaty
of peace made with Germany, which is the model of the
rest.

We shall now proceed by way of commentary on the
Covenant as thus settled, using the first Draft, which is
reprinted in full in the Appendix, so far as may appear
proper to throw light on the choice and significance of the
final text. As the commentary published along with the
text by our Foreign Office may be taken to represent the
views of the Allied Powers, we shall resort to it freely,
referring to it as " the Commentary " without addition.
Quotations made without specific reference are taken from
this document. It is to be noted that the English text of
the Covenant is authentic.

PREAMBLE.

In order to promote international co-operation and to
achieve international peace and security by the acceptance
of obligations not to resort to war, by the prescription of
open, just and honourable relations between nations, by the
firm establishment of the undertakings of international law
as the actual rule of conduct among Governments, and by
the maintenance of justice and a scrupulous respect for all
treaty obligations in the dealings of organised peoples with

(a) Commentary officially published, 1919, Omd. 151, p. 12.

one another, the High Contracting Parties agree to this
Covenant of the League of Nations.

It is officially declared that the Covenant " is not the
constitution of a super-State, but, as its title explains, a
solemn agreement between sovereign States, which consent
to limit their complete freedom of action on certain points
for the greater good of themselves and the world at large.
If the nations of the future are in the main selfish, grasping and warlike, no instrument or machinery will restrain
them.   It is only possible to establish an organisation
which may make peaceful co-operation easy and hence
customary,"—and, we venture to add, breach of the peace
difficult and dangerous—" and to trust in the influence
of custom to mould opinion."   One of the aims declared
in the preamble is " the firm establishment of the undertakings of international law as the actual rule of conduct
among governments."   This involves the affirmation, as
against the insular doctrine lately rather prevalent in
England, that there really is such a thing as international
law, and, as against the Prussian Junkers' doctrine that
the interest of the State overrides all legal and moral
obligation, that its rules when ascertained are binding as
of right (b).   It is just possible to read the word " undertakings " as limiting the law which is to be established
and maintained to the contents of express conventions; but
we can hardly believe that this was the framers' meaning.

(b) There is—need we say it?—a very wide ethical difference
between denying that the law of nations can properly be called
law and denying that any kind of law can be more than a matter
of voluntary usage for the infallible State.

"Covenant." This word has a special solemnity in English; as M. de Lapradelle observed, speaking at Lausanne early in July, 1919, "il y a dans le terme de ' covenant ' ce que l'histoire de Grande-Bretagne y a impliqué de sacré, de religieux." " Pacte " has been chosen for the official French version as being the nearest equivalent.

ARTICLE I.

The original Members of the League of Nations shall be those of the Signatories which are named in the Annex to this Covenant and also such of those other States named in the Annex as shall accede without reservation to this Covenant. Such accession shall be effected by a Declaration deposited with the Secretariat within two months of the coming into force of the Covenant. Notice thereof shall be sent to all other Members of the League.

Any fully self-governing State, Dominion, or Colony not named in the Annex may become a Member of the League if its admission is agreed to by two-thirds of the Assembly, provided that it shall give effective guarantees of its sincere intention to observe its international obligations, and shall accept such regulations as may be prescribed by the League in regard to its military and naval forces and armaments.

Any Member of the League may, after two years' notice of its intention so to do, withdraw from the League, provided that all its international obligations and all its obligations under this Covenant shall have been fulfilled at the time of its withdrawal.

The original signatories, as appears by the annex (p. 174, below), include all the States that were at war with Germany and her allies, with the unfortunate exception of Russia, which at the date of the treaty of peace had no settled government. Of these Czecho-Slovakia, Hedjaz, Poland, and the Serb-Croat-Slovene State, were formed or reconstructed during the war. On the part of the British Empire there were separate signatures for Canada,

Australia, South Africa, New Zealand, and India.   The
representation of India not by the Secretary of State but
by an Indian ruling prince, the Maharaja of Bikanir, deserves to be specially marked. For the future historians of
Indian constitutional development it will be a capital fact.

The position of a State which is a party to a treaty of
peace embodying the Covenant, but is neither an original
member nor one of the States invited to accede, may call
for more exact consideration than is given to it in the
official commentary.   Such a State has conclusive notice
of the Covenant and of its contents, and therein of the
conditions on which new members are admitted.   If it
seeks admission it must do so without reservation of any
kind, and the suggestion of any amendment or variation
is inadmissible; just as every candidate for a club or
society governed by rules is understood to accept the whole
and every part of the rules as they stand at the date of his
election and to submit to all regulations made. by the
committee or other governing body within the authority,
conferred by the rules, and when elected acquires the
ordinary rights of a member, as prescribed by the rules
and not otherwise, to move or promote amendments.   This,
it seems, is the amount of the implied agreement to the
constitution of the League which arises from being a party
to a treaty including it.   But farther, it seems that when
the Covenant stands as part of a more general treaty the
term " the High Contracting Parties," occurring in the
preamble, includes all the parties to the treaty, and is not
confined to the original signatories of the Covenant.   If
this construction be right, every party to the treaty must

be deemed to "agree to this Covenant of the League of
Nations" expressly and not only by implication. But if
not, it does not appear that the practical result is materially different. In either case the parties to the treaty of
peace are all alike bound to recognize the existence of the
League of Nations and the terms on which, if not original
or invited members, they can become so.

It will be specially noted that every joining member
is bound to accept the regulations of the League as to its
armaments of every kind. The effective guarantees of
good faith to be given by a joining member are wisely not
defined beforehand. Not only the existing form of
government, geographical situation and resources of the
candidate Power must be considered, but its previous history and reputation and other relevant circumstances. We
may find a useful analogy in the case, familiar in most
civilized countries, of a club where election is by the
committee. There practice very soon begets a continuous
and flexible tradition which is much more effective than
any set rule could have been. So far as the present
writer's knowledge goes the tendency in such cases is for
the standard to be raised by imperceptible degrees rather
than lowered; whereas it is notorious that the most express
and apparently stringent qualifications imposed by old
written rules have constantly fallen into disregard in all
kinds of public bodies and corporations.

The conditions of membership are substantially the same
as in the Draft, where they are in a less conspicuous place
under Art. 7. Mere variations in the wording or order
of the clauses as between the Draft and the final Covenant

will henceforth not be noticed without some special reason.
The provision for withdrawal from the League at two
years' notice was not in the Draft. It does not seem very
likely to be acted upon; if the League were to break up
it would break in a different fashion, and so long as it
holds firm one can hardly conceive what should make it
desirable for any one State to secede. Nevertheless this
clause is important in so far as it clearly shows that the
League is a concert of independent Powers and not a
federal union, and does not aim at establishing a super-
national government. There is a school of publicists who
may regret this, including some able Americans who know
everything about the higher politics except that Europe
is not America, and the Supreme Court of the United
States is not a pattern that can be reproduced to order.
Peradventure their ideal may become practicable a century
or two hence, unless the whole of our political machinery
has become as obsolete as feudalism, which it may then be
for anything we know. What is certain is that the time
is not ripe at this day for a cosmopolitan federation. It
may be added that the formal ease or difficulty of rescind-
ing a compact has no constant relation whatever to its
stability in practice. Many partnerships at will, many
lettings determinable at half a year's notice or less, many
tenures of offices held at pleasure or renewable at short
intervals, have lasted over a generation or more, as any
man of business can avouch. Let us hope that a hundred
years hence the clerk in charge of the file of withdrawal
notices at the Secretariat of the League may be as hard
to identify as was in the early nineteenth century the clerk

of essoins in the old Court of Common Pleas. On the other hand we know too well that no peace or alliance was ever made perpetual by calling it so, not to speak of marriage or other examples in the sphere of private affairs.

Article II.

The action of the League under this Covenant shall be effected through the instrumentality of an Assembly and of a Council, with a permanent Secretariat.

Here the essential organs of the League are reduced to the simplest possible terms on the lines of Gen. Smuts's forecast. No mention is made of two elements that are prominent in almost every earlier scheme, namely, a permanent court for "justiciable" questions, and a board or council of conciliation for the discussion and adjustment of matters less capable of judicial treatment. As to these, the formation of a tribunal is only postponed; the council is charged with making plans for its establishment, as we shall see in Art. 14. Serious disputes not submitted to the court or to some form of agreed arbitration are to be dealt with by the Council, which may seek an opinion from the court or refer any question to the Assembly (Art. 15). Want of time was the urgent motive, one may presume, for not attempting to make the constitution of the court part of the Covenant itself; but, apart from this, a small council is a much fitter body for such a task than a general meeting of delegates.

In the Draft the Assembly was called a Body of Delegates. The abolition of this clumsy name is a distinct improvement. It was doubtless intended to mark the character of the assembly as being not a world-parliament, but a senate of Powers in which all members of the League are to meet on an equal footing. This, however, is made clear enough by the specific provisions.

There has been a demand in some quarters for an assembly composed in whole or in part of members elected by direct popular representation. Any such demand either belongs to a plan for an entirely different kind of League amounting to a true federation, which, as we have seen, is contrary to the intention of the founders, or springs from radical misapprehension of the principles and usage hitherto recognized in the relations of sovereign States. Independent Powers deal with one another through their governments and not otherwise. The titular rulers of a nation may be bound by a written constitution or by constitutional practice to make treaties only with the concurrence of the legislature or a branch thereof, or with the support of a popular vote; and in such cases it may be necessary for them to make their engagements with other Powers conditional on the proper consent being obtained. But it is not the business of one government to interpret the constitutional limitations of another, or to take notice of them without authentic information. Recognition of a foreign government, even if only as a *de facto* government, implies recognition of its Ministers and diplomatic representatives as authorized agents. Authorities being once verified as in due form, there can be no question of going behind them into matters of domestic politics. As a matter of fact the greatest trouble of diplomatists has often been in dealing with nominally autocratic rulers whom their Ministers had no power to bind, and whose final decision might depend on the person who last had the opportunity of button-holing them. With a parliamentary government one can see the machine at work. But in the strict theory of international law the government of every State is as regards every other State an indivisible and impenetrable monad.

There is nothing, however, to prevent the government of any member of the League from selecting its delegates to the Assembly, or any of them, by some form of direct or indirect popular vote. Only that does not concern the other members. " It is left to the several States to decide how their respective delegations shall be composed; the members need not all be spokesmen of their governments." Lord Robert Cecil has suggested a method of semi-official popular representation outside the Assembly. " The Assembly supplies a real want; there must be some body composed of the representatives of the governments, some conference of the member States, in which official decisions can be taken. But there are strong arguments for having, in addition to the Assembly, a body of the representatives of the popular element in each member country, their method of selection being left to the country concerned. The creation of such a body does not require any amendment of the Covenant; for I do not suggest that this House of Representatives should be given legislative powers. But I do think that by debating and passing resolutions, or even by drafting treaties for the approval of the Assembly, it could do valuable work." With great respect, would not a body of that kind demand a definite share of real power as the condition of doing any real work? Or, if it is to be mainly critical, had it not better be quite un-official?

Some instruction may be derived from the practice of our own courts of justice in cases where the standing of persons or bodies claiming to exercise national rights is called in question. The court does not hear argument on the suggestion of any such doubt, but asks the Secretary of State for Foreign Affairs whom His Majesty's Government recognizes as the sovereign of such and such a territory, or whether it has acknowledged such and such a provisional government as independent; and the answer returned from the Foreign Office is received as conclusive (c).

The constitution of the Secretariat is dealt with in Art. 6.

ARTICLE III.

The Assembly shall consist of Representatives of the Members of the League.

The Assembly shall meet at stated intervals and from time to time as occasion may require at the Seat of the League, or at such other place as may be decided upon.

The Assembly may deal at its meetings with any matter within the sphere of action of the League or affecting the peace of the world.

At meetings of the Assembly each Member of the League shall have one vote, and may have not more than three Representatives.

(c) The personal immunity of reigning princes from legal process in our courts, of which I have lately had occasion to speak elsewhere (Fortn. Rev. Dec. 1918, p. 815), is dealt with in a similar but not exactly the same manner: I mention this here only to avoid confusion. See *Mighell* v. *Sultan of Johore*, [1894] 1 Q. B. 149.

This Article is rather more fully expressed than Art. 2 of the Draft, and, as elsewhere, " Members of the League " takes the place of "High Contracting Parties"; this makes for clearness, though the intention of the Draft that after-admitted members would by their admission become contracting parties on the same footing as original members was not really ambiguous.

The Assembly " will consist of the official representatives of all the members of the League, including the British Dominions and India." One delegate for Great Britain, four for the Dominions, and one for India, make a total of six, while the United States have only one. At first sight this looks like a surprising over-representation of the British Empire in proportion to other Powers. But the seeming anomaly disappears when we consider that this is not the case of an ordinary deliberative assembly deciding questions by a majority. There is really no question of counting votes. "Decisions of the Assembly, except in certain specified cases, must be unanimous," so that no combination can swamp a minority. The practical effect, therefore, is to give the Dominions and India an effective voice, and at need the decisive power of a veto, for the representation and protection of their particular interests and views. No one who is tolerably well acquainted with the political conditions of the British commonwealth of nations, in which a unique form of partnership has been developed under cover of the nominal supremacy reserved to the King in Parliament, is likely to deny that this is only reasonable. What is more, any such man will easily perceive that the statesmen of the

7 (2)

Dominions would not have consented to the British Empire entering into the League of Nations on any other terms. The appearance of India as a co-equal partner with the Dominions is a fact of the first historical importance, but it is beyond the scope of this work to dwell upon its significance or its far-reaching consequences, foreseen and accepted with wisdom for which His Majesty's Government has received too little credit.

It might be supposed offhand that the requirement of unanimity in most matters will make the Assembly a cumbrous and inefficient machine. This would be a great mistake, for the reasons pointed out in the commentary. " At the present stage of national feeling, sovereign States will not consent to be bound by legislation voted by a majority, even an overwhelming majority, of their fellows. But if their sovereignty is respected in theory, it is unlikely that they will permanently withstand a strong consensus of opinion, except in matters which they consider vital." The like reason applies, as we shall presently see, to the Council.

" The Assembly is competent to discuss all matters concerning the League, and it is presumably through the Assembly that the assent of the governments of the world will be given to alterations and improvements in international law (see Art. 19), and to the many conventions that will be required for joint international action."

The Assembly of the League of Nations bears a certain superficial resemblance to the Congress of the United States as it existed under the Articles of Confederation framed in 1777, ratified in 1781, and superseded by the

Constitution of the United States in 1787, a Congress which represented not population but States, with a limited optional number of delegates but only one vote for each State, and exercised or attempted to exercise its ordinary executive functions through a "Committee of the States," in which each State had only one delegate. But, for want of any definite or adequate federal organs, the system of the Articles broke down in a few years; the decisive element was incompetence in matters of interstate commerce, a kind of trouble which even under the Constitution was finally subdued only by the clear head and firm hand of John Marshall. It was too much for a league of sovereign States, and too little for a federation. Comparison, therefore, cannot be undertaken to any profitable end. The text of the Articles as well as of the present Constitution is easy of access, most conveniently perhaps in quite recent British and American publications (d).

Article IV.

The Council shall consist of Representatives of the United States of America, of the British Empire, of France, of Italy, and of Japan, together with Representatives of four other Members of the League. These four Members of the League shall be selected by the Assembly from time to time in its discretion. Until the appointment of the Representatives of the four Members of the League first selected by the Assembly, Representatives of Belgium, Brazil, Greece and Spain shall be Members of the Council.

With the approval of the majority of the Assembly, the Council may name additional Members of the League whose

(d) The Commonwealth of Nations, Part 1, ed. L. Curtis, London, 1916, p. 653. James Madison's Notes of debates in the Federal Convention of 1787, &c., by James Brown Scott, New York, London, &c., 1918, p. 110.

Representatives shall always be members of the Council; the Council with like approval may increase the number of Members of the League to be selected by the Assembly for representation on the Council.

The Council shall meet from time to time as occasion may require, and at least once a year, at the Seat of the League (e), or at such other place as may be decided upon.

The Council may deal at its meetings with any matter within the sphere of action of the League or affecting the peace of the world.

Any Member of the League not represented on the Council shall be invited to send a Representative to sit as a member at any meeting of the Council during the consideration of matters specially affecting the interests of that Member of the League.

At meetings of the Council each Member of the League represented on the Council shall have one vote, and may have not more than one Representative.

The Council is not now called " Executive Council " as it was in the Draft. It will be seen that its normal functions are in truth much more administrative than executive. Nevertheless it is officially described as " a political instrument endowed with greater authority than any the world has hitherto seen. In form its decisions are only recommendations, but when those who recommend include the political chiefs of all the Great Powers and of four other Powers selected by the States of the world in assembly, their unanimous recommendations are likely to be irresistible. . . . The fact that for the decisions of the Council, as of the Assembly, unanimity is ordinarily required (f), is not likely to be a serious obstacle in practice. Granted the desire to agree, which the conception of the League demands, it is believed that agreement will be

(e) Geneva. See Art. 7.
(f) See Art. 5.

reached, or at least that the minority will acquiesce. There would be little practical advantage, and a good deal of danger, in allowing the majority of the Council to vote down one of the Great Powers. An important exception to the rule of unanimity is made by the clause in Art. 15 providing that, in the case of disputes submitted to the Council, the consent of the parties is not required to make its recommendations valid." Such a recommendation, however, is not to have any automatic effect, as we shall see in considering that Article.

As to voting power, the remarks made under Art. 3 on the constitution of the Assembly are no less applicable to the Council. Except in certain particular cases (see Art. 5) decisions must be unanimous, and therefore no Power need fear being outvoted. Both in formal debate and in the informal conversations that will precede it, the weight of any Power's representatives will not depend on their number, but partly on their personal character and partly on the extent to which they can assure their colleagues that they express the true mind of their respective nations.

" The relations between the Assembly and the Council are purposely left undefined, as it is held undesirable to limit the competence of either. Cases will arise when a meeting of the Assembly would be inconvenient, and the Council should not therefore be bound to wait on its approval." It is probable, as the Commentary goes on to observe, that the members of the Council will also have seats in the Assembly; the risk of accidental overlapping may therefore be neglected.

Admission of new members to the League is already provided for in Art. 1, par. 2, but a Power admitted under that clause will not thereby become entitled to representation on the Council. Discretion in that respect is entrusted by the second paragraph of the present Article to the Council itself, with the approval of a majority of the Assembly. A joining member, if of sufficient importance, may acquire standing representation, or if it is not of the first rank an increase in the number of selected members will enable the Assembly to give it a representative without prejudice to the choices already made. The cases contemplated as probable in the near future are, as the Commentary points out, those of Germany and Russia. This does not mean, of course, that the founders of the League warrant the existence of an internationally honest government in Germany, or of a stable government in Russia, within the next few months. Whatever some people may expect of them, they do not profess to be gods or prophets.

It is obviously of great importance that all the members of the League, and especially the smaller Powers, should have confidence in the Council, and that decisions affecting the interest of any member should not be made without notice and an opportunity of being heard. The last paragraph but one of this Article gives not only the assurance of notice and opportunity, but an actual seat and effective voice in the Council for the time being; for the invited representative of any Power, not being already represented on the Council, whose interests are affected, is to sit *as a member*. The constitution of the British Imperial

Defence Committee and the recent usage of the Imperial War Cabinet may perhaps have suggested this very useful provision. Everyone summoned to those bodies was summoned not as an assessor, but as a full member, whether his attendance was habitual or occasional, or only for some special cause that might not recur.

ARTICLE V.

Except where otherwise expressly provided in this Covenant, decisions at any meeting of the Assembly or of the Council shall require the agreement of all the Members of the League represented at the meeting.

All matters of procedure at meetings of the Assembly or of the Council, including the appointment of Committees to investigate particular matters, shall be regulated by the Assembly or by the Council, and may be decided by a majority of the Members of the League represented at the meeting.

The first meeting of the Assembly and the first meeting of the Council shall be summoned by the President of the United States of America.

The exceptional cases in which a majority vote may have effect are the following:—

Admission of new members to the League. Two-thirds majority of the Assembly (Art. 1).

Approval of new members named by the Council to have permanent representatives thereon, and of increase in number of members selected for a share of representation. Majority of Assembly (Art. 4).

Procedure. Majority of members represented at meeting of Assembly or Council (Art. 5, above). This is the only ordinary case in which the Council need not be unanimous.

Approval of future appointments of Secretary-General by Council. Majority of Assembly (Art. 6).

Disputes referred to Council. Report may be by a majority vote: likewise in the Assembly where the reference is passed on to it by the Council (Art. 15).

Exclusion from the League for breach of covenant. Representatives of all other members represented on the Council (not only at the particular meeting) (Art. 16).

Ratification of amendments to the Covenant. Majority of Powers represented in the Assembly. All represented in the Council must concur (Art. 26).

It will be seen that at any meeting any member of the League may give a merely passive assent, signifying either indifference or unwilling acquiescence (like that of a judge who does not wholly agree with the majority of the court but does not formally dissent), by abstaining from attendance at the meeting. Such cases are not likely to be frequent or important, and the provision that the agreement of members represented at the meeting shall be sufficient appears to be inserted rather for the innocent purpose of expediting business and preventing abstention from being used as an instrument of obstructive delay in minor matters. If on questions of procedure an absolute majority of the constituent Powers were required, it would be possible for a small discontented group, whose reasons would not bear examination in open debate, to give considerable trouble by hindering the formation of a quorum. In the matters of substance where the members represented at the meeting must be unanimous it is obvious that to require the consent of every member of the League, present

or not, would be to give every one of them, from the
greatest to the least, not only a veto but an arbitrary
veto exercisable without assigning any reason. Again, it
was obviously not desirable that the proceedings should be
liable to frustration by unavoidable accident keeping the
representatives of one or two members away, which, though
not very likely, is not impossible. In any case the wilful
absence of any Great Power's representatives from the
discussion of a serious question is hardly to be thought of.
If such a thing happened it would be a signal of something very dangerous in the state of the League. Against
radical discords, whether already latent, or even known to
be threatening but not remediable at the time (as the conflict of free and slave States in North America), or such as
may arise from unsuspected causes in the future, there
is no safeguard in any written constitution; and the only
superiority of an unwritten one, if indeed it has enough
substance to count for much except among men in love
with formulas, is that it is somewhat easier to disguise
revolutionary changes with a show of legality, as was done
in England in 1688.

We may read in this Article a general intention that the
current business of the League shall be transacted mainly
through committees appointed from time to time, standing
or transitory according to the nature of the case. It is
also possible that the meetings of the Council or the Assembly which put such affairs in train may themselves
resemble committee meetings in substance though not in
form. A full attendance may be thought needless when
the administrative details to be settled involve no question

of principle; and in such cases it may come to be understood that, while every member will have notice and will
be entitled to attend, it is in practice left to the Secretariat to ensure a competent quorum.   Any such working
arrangement implies, of course, large confidence in the
Secretary-General's judgment and tact.   That, however,
is already assumed in the constitution of the Secretariat
and the functions entrusted to it.   A mediocre departmental officer with a staff of ordinary clerks would either
tie up the League in red tape or get its routine into an
inextricable tangle.

ARTICLE VI.

The permanent Secretariat shall be established at the Seat
of the League.   The Secretariat shall comprise a Secretary-
General and such secretaries and staff as may be required.

The first Secretary-General shall be the person named in
the Annex; thereafter the Secretary-General shall be appointed by the Council with the approval of the majority
of the Assembly.

The secretaries and the staff of the Secretariat shall be
appointed by the Secretary-General with the approval of
the Council.

The Secretary-General shall act in that capacity at all
meetings of the Assembly and of the Council.

The expenses of the Secretariat shall be borne by the
Members of the League in accordance with the apportion-
ment of the expenses of the International Bureau of the
Universal Postal Union.

The person named in the Annex is Sir James Eric
Drummond.

" A link between the two bodies "—the Assembly and
the Council—" is supplied by the permanent Secretariat,
or new international Civil Service.   This organisation has
immense possibilities of usefulness, and a very wide field

will be open for the energy and initiative of the first
Secretary-General. One of the most important of his
duties will be the collection, sifting, and distribution of
information from all parts of the world. A reliable supply
of facts and statistics will in itself be a powerful aid to
peace. Nor can the value be exaggerated of the continuous
collaboration of experts and officials in matters tending to
emphasize the unity, rather than the diversity of national
interests." It had already been inferred from the Draft
at an earlier stage that the Secretariat was intended to
be the working centre of the League, and the Secretary-
General would be a very important officer. This passage
of the Commentary makes the inference explicit and
authoritative.

I cannot help observing, though it is not strictly relevant here, that the formation of a secretariat and a general
intelligence department for the British Empire on very
much the same lines has been urged on successive British
governments for about fifteen years; but by reason, it is
believed, of stubborn departmental obstruction in the
Colonial Office, next to nothing was done before the war.
The formation of the Imperial War Cabinet put matters
on a new footing, of which we may hope to see the fruit
in due time, after the pressing business of the peace
treaties is disposed of. As the reasons given in the Commentary are perfectly applicable to the relations between
Great Britain and the Dominions, it will at least be hard
to maintain that a scheme which all the Great Powers
regard as practicable and highly important for the League
of Nations is less practicable or desirable in our own

affairs. It must be allowed that in this, as in all matters of the higher politics, the ignorance and indifference of British electors and their representatives in Parliament have much to answer for.

ARTICLE VII.

The Seat of the League is established at Geneva.

The Council may at any time decide that the Seat of the League shall be established elsewhere.

All positions under or in connection with the League, including the Secretariat, shall be open equally to men and women.

Representatives of the Members of the League and officials of the League when engaged on the business of the League shall enjoy diplomatic privileges and immunities.

The buildings and other property occupied by the League or its officials or by Representatives attending its meetings shall be inviolable.

It is not likely that we shall see a woman Secretary-General of the League in our time, but the assertion of the principle marks the change which has come over public opinion as to women's capacity during the war. There is no need to dwell here on the achievements of women in fields of manual and intellectual work, or combinations of both, that were supposed to be fit only for men, or on the skill, devotion, and courage with which they have performed their duties under the hardest conditions and through trials of the most searching kind. But in the present connexion it may be noted that very many women have been employed by our Departments in highly confidential dealings with enemy correspondence and the like, and have shown themselves quite as trustworthy as men in keeping official secrets.

The suggestion of a distinct women's section in the Secretariat made by some societies appears to me, as it does to the French National Council of Women, to be misconceived (*g*).

There has been unofficial talk of reconsidering the decision to fix the seat of the League at Geneva. As to this it should be observed that the only serious alternative was to choose Brussels, and Belgium was a party to the decision. Moreover the nomination was promptly welcomed by the Canton of Geneva in a proclamation issued at the end of A'pril, 1919; the language of the Cantonal Council of State is not only cordial but enthusiastic (*h*). It will be enough to translate here one paragraph, which is less warm if anything than most of the context: "Geneva, with her continuous history of combats for independence, will take a just pride in welcoming the men who within her walls will pass judgment on the independence of nations." After this one does not see how the League could go back upon its choice without grave incivility towards the governments both of the Canton and of the Swiss Confederation.

(*g*) See The League of Nations Journal, Sept., 1919, at p. 331.
(*h*) Full text in "The League of Nations," Berne, No. 4, May 10th, 1919.

CHAPTER VI.

RESTRAINT OF WAR.

ARTICLE VIII.

The Members of the League recognise that the maintenance of peace requires the reduction of national armaments to the lowest point consistent with national safety and the enforcement by common action of international obligations.

The Council, taking account of the geographical situation and circumstances of each Member of the League, shall formulate plans for such reduction for the consideration and action of the several Governments.

Such plans shall be subject to reconsideration and revision at least every ten years.

After these plans shall have been adopted by the several Governments, the limits of armaments therein fixed shall not be exceeded without the concurrence of the Council.

The Members of the League agree that the manufacture by private enterprise of munitions and implements of war is open to grave objections. The Council shall advise how the evil effects attendant upon such manufacture can be prevented, due regard being had to the necessities of those Members of the League which are not able to manufacture the munitions and implements of war necessary for their safety.

The Members of the League undertake to interchange full and frank information as to the scale of their armaments, their military and naval programmes, and the condition of such of their industries as are adaptable to war-like purposes.

" THERE is to be no dictation by the Council or anyone else as to the size of national forces. The Council is merely to formulate plans, which the governments are free to accept or reject. Once accepted, the members agree not to exceed them. The formulation and acceptance of such plans may be expected to take shape in a general Disarmament Convention, supplementary to the Covenant."

So the Commentary explains the spirit of this Article. If anyone thinks the framers of the Covenant have been unduly timid, let him consider that at least they have succeeded in lifting the matter out of the slough of despond where, to all appearance, two Peace Conferences had left it.

Disarmament was intended to be the principal object of the first Hague Conference in 1899. So far from coming within sight of any convention or general understanding concerning the limitation of armaments, the Conference wholly failed to produce any appreciable result, and its credit was saved only at a late stage by the creation of the Hague Tribunal, which had been no part of the original plan.

At the second Conference in 1907, the German Government appointed delegates only on condition of the limitation of armaments not being among the heads of discussion. That was twelve years ago, no great lapse of time in any normal circumstances, according to the usual measure of international movements. But even if the subject had not been banned it is hard to see how a large and miscellaneous meeting, in which no really confidential exchange of views and information was possible, could have arrived at any satisfactory result. The only hopeful way would have been to appoint a special and secret committee to inquire and report. It would be idle curiosity to consider at this day whether the Conference would have agreed to set up such a committee, if it had been free to do so, or whether

P. 8

the time at the committee's disposal would have allowed
it to arrive at conclusions of any value.

We now have the Council of the League, a body within
which the necessary confidential preliminaries are practicable, charged with making plans for the reduction of
armaments in its own time. That is at any rate a reasonable method. How soon it can be put in operation depends
on the restoration of settled government (not meaning
thereby any return to political systems resembling those
which have been cleared away) in eastern and central
Europe. So long as the late Russian, German, and
Austro-Hungarian Empires are for the most part represented by unknown quantities, the materials for framing
a comparative scale of armaments are not at hand.
Obviously the Council will not commit itself to the official
formulation of any scheme for limitation of armaments,
general or partial, without some previous assurance that
the Powers to whom it will be addressed are disposed to
accept and act upon it in substance. As these Powers are
in practice pretty sure to be represented on the Council
itself, there ought to be no difficulty about this. It is
earnestly to be hoped that the contents of the confidential
and sometimes delicate communications that must take
place at the meetings of the Council or at the Secretariat
will be kept out of the field of parliamentary questionings
and journalistic gossip. Clients do not expect to be present
at all their solicitors' interviews; if they were foolish
enough to demand it, and made their claim good, the
volume of litigation would be disastrously multiplied, and
the number of failures to complete business of every kind

even more so. Already there have been too many so-called revelations about the intimate proceedings of the Peace Conference at Paris.

There are great difficulties about the regulation of private enterprise in the production of war material. It must be remembered that this is by no means confined to guns and ammunition. A highly important part of it is the building of warships, which are certainly implements of war though not immediately suggested by the term. To forbid minor maritime States to buy their vessels, or some of them, from foreign building yards would be to condemn them to new and heavy expense; and after all the result would probably be that in almost every case one of the great firms would set up a local branch under an official title. The work, in its higher branches at any rate, and the profits, would be very much as they were before, and the cost of production would be increased. It would be absurd, again, to say to a former customer of a firm prepared to supply both ship and armament: "You may get your ship where you please, but not the guns with it." Whereupon the question would arise whether gun-mountings should be reckoned as part of the ship or accessory to the gun, and probably other technical questions that any naval constructor could easily suggest. Then, as regards ships as well as arms and munitions generally, the effect of suppressing private enterprise would be either to multiply centres of production and increase the difficulties of ascertaining how much they produced, or to make minor Powers customers to the State arsenals of the greater maritime and military Powers, and thus in effect create a system of

8 (2)

particular dependent alliances which would be fraught
with danger to the future harmony of the League and the
peace of the world.

In short the people who have been talking glibly about
suppressing private traffic in the instruments of war have
not thought seriously before speaking, or, if they have,
were unable to escape from a long acquired habit of thinking in a strictly parochial manner. The same remark
applies to compulsory service, of which there will be a
word to say presently.

This is not to deny that unlimited traffic in deadly
weapons, military or other, explosives, poisons and other
dangerous goods is not tolerable in any civilized country,
and control must be exercised (as in many respects it is
already) by pretty strong domestic legislation. Neither
is it denied that some measure of general regulation under
the direction of the League of Nations is desirable, and
with diligence and caution may be accomplished. The
ultimate remedy, however, is not in checking the production of instruments of war, but in removing the causes
of fear and mistrust that lead to excessive armaments. A
syndicate of all the armament factories in the world could
not force its wares on nations who did not want them.

Proposals have been made from time to time for the
mechanical limitation of armaments, as one may call it.
Under such a scheme vessels of war, for example, might
not exceed a certain tonnage, or guns a certain calibre.
We do not think this method is within the range of practical discussion. Certainly there is no chance of the
members of the League of Nations agreeing to any such

restrictions at present; moreover it seems gravely doubtful whether, if practicable, they would tend to prevent war or to make it less destructive of human life. I know of no reason to believe that casualties were lighter than they are now, in proportion to the numbers engaged, in the days when men fought with primitive or comparatively rude weapons; indeed, I believe the evidence is the other way. But an effective comparison would have to be made not between losses in particular combats, but between the proportion of combatant casualties which in the wars or campaigns under review had to be suffered for the attainment of definite military results; and here the enormous length of ancient wars (though it was due probably to a rudimentary condition of the art of war rather than to imperfect instruments) would have to be reckoned with. It would lead us too far to pursue this by-path even if I had the necessary special competence (a).

Here there is a possible confusion to be avoided. From the earliest historical times the usage of civilized warfare has forbidden the use of certain means of offence, poison being the most familiar example, not with any view to the prevention or discouragement of war, but on grounds of humanity and of a dignity and decency of conduct to be observed even between enemies. The governing principle is that the immediate object in war is to disable one's

---

(a) I do not know from what date (a modern one, I suspect) trustworthy figures are attainable, or deaths in action distinguishable from the losses by sickness and want of proper medical service which we have seen reduced to relatively insignificant dimensions.

enemy (not necessarily to kill him, as indeed a wounded
man is more of a hindrance to his own side for the time
being than a dead one), and whatever exceeds this purpose
by inflicting incurable or needlessly painful injuries is
unworthy of honourable combatants, and such practices
little better, if more tolerable at all, than deliberate
slaughter of prisoners, unresisting wounded men, or non-
combatants.   There is nothing new in this; the Homeric
poems show that the use of poisoned arrows was disallowed
among Greek warriors before the text was settled in
its present form, though, it seems, the disallowance was
not then very old (b).

The Hague Conventions defined and in some details
reinforced these customary prohibitions; but in the war
of 1914 the German commanders, while they were vehe-
ment in denouncing breaches of the Conventions on the

(b) Near the beginning of the Odyssey Athena in the assumed
character of Mentes tells a story of Odysseus having begged for
poison for his arrows from a man who refused "because he
feared the wrath of the immortal gods"; but another and older
man gave it him as a special favour. It is clear, however, that
the arrows Odysseus uses to kill the suitors are not poisoned;
there is no suggestion of it in the text. In the poet's time,
therefore, the modern rule was already settled. The fuss made
over a mere scratch from an arrow in Il. iv., 139 *sqq.*, points
to an earlier time when arrows were presumed to be poisoned
(it was a Trojan arrow, but the Homeric Trojans are no bar-
barians though they have barbarous auxiliaries); the story of
Philoctetes is another archaic survival, tolerated in classical
literature as belonging to a world of magic in which all things
are possible. Poisoned weapons were apparently forbidden by
Indian custom from a no less early time: Manu, vii., 90. See
Gilbert Murray, The Rise of the Greek Epic, p. 120.

part of the Allies, mostly or indeed wholly fictitious,
openly followed in their own practice the opinion already
proclaimed under the auspices of the Prussian General
Staff, that the laws of war are only voluntary observances
which may and ought to be disregarded if any considerable
military advantage can be gained thereby.   The Allies
were compelled to retaliate in self-defence, and with such
effect that before the end of the war the Germans were
probably rather sorry for their invention of gas attacks.
One of the first constructive duties of the League of
Nations will be to restore the ideals of civilized warfare,
define them with increased clearness, and provide effectual
means for enforcing them if the need should arise.

" The exchange of information stipulated for in the last
paragraph of the Article will, no doubt, be effected through
the Commission mentioned in Article 9.   The suggestion
that this Commission might be given a general power of
inspection and supervision, in order to ensure the observance of Article 8, was rejected for several reasons.   In the
first place, such a power would not be tolerated by many
national States at the present day, but would cause friction
and hostility to the idea of the League; nor, in fact, is it
in harmony with the assumption of mutual good faith on
which the League is founded, seeing that the members
agree to exchange full and frank information; nor, finally,
would it really be of practical use.   Preparations for war
on a large scale cannot be concealed, while no inspection
could hope to discover such really important secrets as
new gases and explosives, and other inventions of detail.
The experience of our own Factory Acts shows what an

army of officials is required to make inspection efficient, and how much may escape observation even then. In any case, the League would certainly receive no better information on such points of detail from a Commission than that obtained through their ordinary intelligence services by the several States." So far the Commentary. The French amendment which will be mentioned under the next Article did not propose to confer powers of official inspection.

This paragraph develops a suggestion made at the Peace Conference of 1907, of which something came but not much. In 1911 Germany agreed to exchange naval programmes with Great Britain; I do not know to what extent this was acted upon, or whether similar action was taken by any other Powers. It may be still doubtful whether the intelligence departments of the leading Powers will really be much wiser than they were before. The real value of the clause is that it sets a standard of good faith and fellowship. Any member of the League who made secret preparations for war, direct or indirect, would thereby commit an express breach of the Covenant. Moreover the Secretary-General and his staff are hereby fully entitled, though not ordered, to keep their eyes open.

Nothing is said about compulsory service here or elsewhere in the Covenant, and the reason is obvious. The military systems of Continental nations, I believe without material exception, are founded on a general civic duty of training and service in one form or another, and they cannot be expected to commit themselves to radical change, even by the most vague and dilatory assertion of a general desire, until the working of the League has stood the test of experience for some considerable time. Great Britain is quite unlike other Powers in her military needs and the tradition founded on them. A voluntary professional army became a matter not of choice but of necessity when expeditions to remote parts of the world and the maintenance of garrisons in India and at many stations over-seas had to be provided for. As to the defence of the realm and the preservation of the peace at home, the public duty of bearing arms for these purposes has always been recognized by the common law, and was always distinct from special services incident to military tenure. Sea power has enabled us, until the extraordinary demands of the late war came, to make that duty a very light one in practice, but it has never been abandoned. For European expeditions it sufficed in the Middle Ages to compose a mixed body of feudal contingents and mercenaries, the latter often foreign, which had no permanent framework and was dispersed when the business was over; and jealousy of the royal power caused politicians to cling to this idea long after it was obsolete, so that to this day the existence of a British army in time of peace and the King's authority to maintain its discipline depend on the passing of an annual Act. Curiously enough the constitutional objection to a standing army belonged in the first half of the eighteenth century to the political stock in trade not of the Whig, but of the Tory party. These familiar facts are mentioned only to remind the reader how far apart we stand from the other nations of Europe both in the nature of our military needs and in the methods, affected only in detail by political reasons and prejudice, by which we have dealt with them. It may be added that the late German form of universal service was fitted only for European war in fields accessible by land from the German frontiers. When the Germans undertook to furnish a contingent to the composite army engaged in the " Boxer " campaign in China, and when they had to deal with a rebellion in South-West Africa, their normal military system was inapplicable, and in each case they were driven to make up a special expeditionary force by voluntary enlistment, it is believed with rather indifferent success.

After the American Civil War the War Department of the United States reverted to its old plan of a quite small voluntary Federal army, supplemented in a rather loose fashion by the militia of the several States in the event of war, and supplementing it at need in time of peace. That precedent, it seems fairly certain, will not now be followed, but there are no materials at present for predicting what the new model of the American army will be like.

On the whole it is clear that the subject is in no way ripe for the League of Nations to take in hand.

A proposed French amendment to the last paragraph is mentioned under the following Article.

ARTICLE IX.

A permanent Commission shall be constituted to advise the Council on the execution of the provisions of Articles I. and VIII. and on military, naval and air questions generally.

This Article has purposely stopped short of creating a

real 'General Staff for the League, and an amendment proposed by the French Government for the purpose of strengthening it was not adopted.   In the final text " Council " replaces " League," and the words " and air " have been added.   " The function of a General Staff," says the Commentary, " is preparation for war, and the latter requires the envisagement of a definite enemy.   It would plainly be impossible for British officers to take part in concerting plans, however hypothetical, against their own country, with any semblance of reality; and all the members of a staff must work together with complete confidence.   It is further evident that no State would communicate to its potential enemies the information as to its own strategic plans necessary for a concerted scheme of defence.   The most that can be done in this direction by the Commission is to collect non-confidential information of military value, and possibly to work out certain transit questions of a special character."

Such is the British and, it may be presumed, also the American view; and the reasons are plausibly stated.   But the manifest fact that the French Government, doubtless advised by its own General Staff, thought otherwise is enough to show that a different opinion is arguable.   It may be conceded that a cosmopolitan staff could not study beforehand the precise measures to be taken against a hypothetical defiance of the League by a rebellious minority.   Besides the patriotic objection, as it may be called, which is frankly stated in the Commentary, the character, possible extent, and military aims of any such resistance must depend on unforeseen political combinations as well as the standing geographical and strategic elements of the problem. Allowing for all this, it remains to be seen whether a sharp line can really be drawn between the functions of a military intelligence department, which the Article as it stands undoubtedly does create, and those of a general staff. The military questions, it must be observed, are much simplified by the provisions of Article 16, which decrees an automatic suspension of all commercial relations in the event of any member of the League resorting to war in disregard of its obligations. Short of a rupture that would destroy the League altogether, the commercial sanction ought to be strong enough in almost any conceivable case, and the consequent military dispositions would be of a merely local and auxiliary kind. We shall touch on this question again under Article 16.

It must also be remembered that Art. 1 expressly enables any member of the League to withdraw from it in a peaceable manner by giving two years' notice.

Taking the text of the present Article as it stands, there is a very practical question as to the duty of the Commission to advise the Council. Is the Commission to wait for the Council to lay specific points before it, or is it to proceed at once to study "the execution of the provisions of Articles 1 and 8" and submit a report or series of reports? The course to be taken in this respect will depend on the intimate relations of the Commission with the Council and the Secretariat. It may not matter very much whether the results are formally presented as answers to requisitions, or as reports founded on the larger interpretation which would read the Article itself as an operative general instruction. But it is certain that unless the Commission is encouraged to do continuous and systematic work (or unless the air of Geneva has a singular gift of inspiring public virtue, which it would be rash to assume), the work it does when its advice is called for at odd times will be of no great value. In the days before Mr. Balfour established the flexible and efficient Imperial Defence Committee there was talk of a Defence Committee of the Cabinet, of which no one could say with certainty whether it had ever met. The Secretary-General will doubtless look to it that there are no such shadowy committees haunting the offices of the League of Nations.

It would seem desirable (to speak with some diffidence in a matter of administrative detail) that the Secretary-General should be the permanent secretary of this Commission, with such expert assistance as he may require. This appears the most natural way of keeping the Commission in touch with the Council; that it should be done in some way is obvious.

The French position as to Articles 8 and 9 has been set forth by M. Léon Bourgeois in the special French number of the *Times* published on Sept. 6, 1919:

"The conditions considered by France to be indispensable were as follows: first, that the armaments of each State should be limited to the figure strictly necessary to assure internal order; secondly, that the contingents required from each State for the establishment of the international force should be so proportioned that the final word should rest with that force in every case; lastly,

France desired that this international force should be kept
in such a state of efficiency that it could suppress any
attempt at aggression with sureness and promptitude.

"The French Delegation therefore submitted to the
Peace Conference two amendments of the greatest
importance:—

"Art. 8.—The High Contracting Parties being determined to interchange full and frank information as to
the scale of their armaments, their military and naval
programmes, and the condition of such of their industries
as are adaptable to warlike purposes, will appoint a
committee for the purpose of ascertaining the necessary
information.

"Art. 9.—A permanent organization shall be set up
for the purpose of providing for and preparing the military and naval measures for enforcing the obligations
which the present Covenant imposes upon the High Contracting Parties and making them immediately effective
in all cases of urgency (c).

"For reasons of greater importance no vote was taken,

(c) It may be convenient to give the French text:—

Art. 8. Les hautes puissances contractantes, résolues à se
donner franche et pleine connaissance mutuelle de l'échelle de
leurs armements et leurs programmes militaires et navals, ainsi
que des conditions de leurs industries susceptibles de s'adapter
à la guerre, institueront une commission chargée des constatations
nécessaires.

Art. 9. Un organisme permanent sera constitué pour prévoir
et préparer les moyens militaires et navals d'exécution des obligations que la présente convention impose aux hautes puissances
contractantes, et pour en assurer l'efficacité immédiate dans tous
les cas d'urgence.

and the text presented by the Commission had to be considered as adopted unanimously."

These amendments, not having been formally rejected, " will certainly come up again at the first meetings of the League of Nations, and when that time arrives France will be by no means alone in upholding them."

Finally M. Bourgeois observes: " It has been said very justly that the greatest force upon which the League of Nations can rely is that of an enlightened public opinion. How can public opinion be informed and how can it act, if no preliminary measures of control and preparation are enacted?"

ARTICLE X.

The Members of the League undertake to respect and preserve as against external aggression the territorial integrity and existing political independence of all Members of the League. In case of any such aggression or in case of any threat or danger of such aggression the Council shall advise upon the means by which this obligation shall be fulfilled.

Here the words " as against external aggression " are of the first importance, showing, as the Commentary says, "that the League cannot be used as a Holy Alliance to suppress national or other movements within the boundaries of the member States, but only to prevent forcible annexation from without." It seems that armed intervention by one member State in the domestic troubles of another, such an interference, for example, as that of Nicolas I. of Russia in Hungary in 1849, or of the restored French monarchy against the constitutional party in Spain, would be an external aggression within the meaning of this Article; and it would make no difference whether the action so taken were in support of or against the established government. The League does not prescribe or recommend any particular form of government, much less guarantee to its members the continuance of existing forms. Every member is sovereign in its own affairs, and answerable to the League only for having some kind of settled government capable of appointing fit representatives for the common business. In the event of internal troubles rising to the height of a conflict between organized bodies maintaining themselves as *de facto* governments and acting as regular belligerents, or indeed when they had gone so far as manifestly *to* threaten such consequences, the case would be such an emergency as the next following Article contemplates. A civil war on a scale involving blockade of ports and interruption of international commerce could not be regarded as of merely domestic concern. But mere transitory and local disturbances, even if they call for the use of considerable military force on the spot, are not in themselves the League's business.

In the second sentence the words are " the Council shall *advise* "—not prescribe. They are plain enough, but there is a disposition in some quarters to ignore them. Some Americans are afraid of the United States being compelled under this Article to do police work in Europe or Asia which may be foreign to American interests. They forget that the United States has a permanent place and voice in the Council, that nothing can be done without the unanimous advice of the Council, and that even then

the Council has no compulsory power. We have even
seen an apprehension expressed that Canada might be
called upon to join in operations against Great Britain.
Such fears are, to speak frankly, midsummer madness.
Still less is there any interference with any constitutional
provision in any member State requiring the consent of
the legislature to a declaration of war (d).

"It is important that this Article should be read with
Articles 11 and 19" (this last provides for reconsideration
of obsolete treaties), "which make it plain that the Covenant is not intended to stamp the new territorial settlement as sacred and unalterable for all time, but, on the
contrary, to provide machinery for the progressive regulation of international affairs in accordance with the needs
of the future. The absence of such machinery, and the
consequent survival of treaties long after they had become
out of date, led to many of the quarrels of the past; so
that these Articles may be said to inaugurate a new international order, which should eliminate, so far as possible,
one of the principal causes of war." Certain critics have
been trying to excite prejudice against the League by
representing it as no better than a new Holy Alliance.
The very plain repudiation of any such tendency by the
Commentary is no doubt designed for the rebuke of these
alarmist fancies, and should be sufficient for the purpose.
Some of these critics belong to that old school of political
sentiment which cherishes a general presumption against
the right of any established government to exist. If they

(d) As to the action of the U. S. Senate since this sheet has
been in print, see the note added to the Preface.

P.   9

expected the League of Nations to be the organ of that
frame of mind their disappointment is inevitable. The
League must be a league of governments and not of revolutionary oppositions. Other objectors are particularists
moved by jealousy for the rights of minor Powers. As
against these it must be said, at the risk of repetition,
that the only alternative to the League is a return to the
system of group alliances that has already proved a failure.
If this did come back the second state would be worse
than the first. Every nation not of the first rank would
practically be driven to attach itself as a satellite to one
of the rival groups; for the notion that minor Powers
alone could form a group of their own strong enough to
hold the balance may be dismissed as chimerical. Then
there are the impenitent militarists, for whom any stick
is good enough to beat the League with, and with whom
it is useless to argue.

ARTICLE XI.

Any war or threat of war, whether immediately affecting
any Members of the League or not, is hereby declared a
matter of concern to the whole League, and the League
shall take any action that may be deemed wise and effectual
to safeguard the peace of nations. In case any such emergency should arise, the Secretary-General shall, on the request of any Member of the League, forthwith summon a
meeting of the Council.

It is also declared to be the friendly right of each Member
of the League to bring to the attention of the Assembly or
of the Council any circumstance whatever affecting international relations which threatens to disturb international
peace or the good understanding between nations upon which
peace depends.

This Article is of the first importance and of exceedingly
wide scope. It has been strengthened in the final recension; in particular the power of any member of the League

to cause a Council meeting to be summoned was not in the Draft. Quite apart from the specific procedure outlined in Articles 12—15, the League is hereby invested, in case of any apparent danger to the general peace, with a large authority which can be exercised, according to the nature of the case, by inquiry, free conference, mediation, or timely warning to any Power outside the League.

Various Irish writers, including some who deserve serious attention, have raised the question whether the standing problem of Irish autonomy can come before the League of Nations. There is only one way in which this could happen, namely, that the Government of the United States should declare Irish-American sympathy with unsatisfied nationalist claims in Ireland to be capable of disturbing good understanding between Great Britain and the United States. That is a possible event if a solution is not reached within a reasonable time, but it is more likely that a confidential intimation from the United States would not only precede a formal reference to the Council but avoid the necessity for it.

Meanwhile it is clear that a deputation to the League of Nations from Dublin in support of a Dominion constitution, or from Cork in support of an Irish Republic, or from Belfast protesting against any kind of Home Rule, would be altogether out of order and could not be received. The League can have no direct dealings with parties or national fractions; it is exempt by its constitution from the temptation which has beset too many British (e) Governments to ally themselves with one sec-

(e) British, not English. For two centuries the people of

tion against another instead of acting for the welfare of the whole.

In the old state of Europe there were two, and so far as I am aware only two partial remedies for a threatening situation, short of war itself, the *ultima ratio regum* insolently flaunted in the common inscription to be seen on Prussian guns. These were the formation of defensive alliances or understandings, and the convocation of a European Congress. The former was a makeshift at best, and aggravated instead of relieving the burden and the danger of competing armaments. The latter could be and more than once was frustrated by the dissent of any one Great Power. We now have a comprehensive, flexible, and we may almost add automatic method for securing ventilation and discussion of European "questions," as the current euphemism ran, and for cutting short any attempts at secret combinations.

Even more than the other operative provisions, this one postulates good will and businesslike determination on the part of at least a working majority, and continuous vigilance and efficiency on the part of the Secretariat. This is only to say once more that, while a covenant can create instruments of action, it cannot create nor does it pretend to create the men who are to act. But finding the necessary instrument ready to hand makes all the difference when time is of the essence. It cannot be too

Scotland have had their full share of power and responsibility for the affairs of the three kingdoms. Talk of any special hostility of "England" is an Irish legend, though Irish Nationalists and Unionists agree in the one point of denying that any Englishman or Scotsman can understand Irishmen.

often repeated that the aim of the League is not to make war wholly impossible, but to make wars of surprise impracticable and to dissipate gathering war-clouds betimes. Consider what would have been the gain to humanity if anything like the scheme of this Article, even in a much cruder form, had been available when war was in sight in 1870 or in 1914. Neither of those wars could have been started in the face of a standing council of the Powers to whom the dispute could have been referred without the delay of preliminary negotiation. Again, the causes of the war of 1914 might have been averted if Russia had been definitely entitled to call the attention of the Powers to the oppression of Slavonic populations under Magyar rule as likely to disturb friendly relations between Austria-Hungary and Russia, which in fact it notoriously did.

The Covenant now proceeds to set up the machinery for dealing with specific disputes. We shall see that a wide and elastic discretion is left in justiciable matters to the parties and in others to the Council. Critics of the school that loves cut and dry formulas will no doubt complain of vagueness, but to the present writer's mind this is among the chief merits of the scheme.

CHAPTER VII.

JUDICIAL PROCESS AND SANCTIONS.

ARTICLE XII.

The Members of the League agree that if there should arise between them any dispute likely to lead to a rupture, they will submit the matter either to arbitration or to inquiry by the Council, and they agree in no case to resort to war until three months after the award by the arbitrators or the report by the Council.

In any case under this Article the award of the arbitrators shall be made within a reasonable time, and the report of the Council shall be made within six months after the submission of the dispute.

HERE a general principle is laid down which the next three following Articles work out. The action to be taken by the League under Article 11 would obviously cover, in an appropriate case, advising the parties to submit the matter for arbitration or inquiry under the present Article. If, however, a dangerous dispute should arise without warning, then the parties are bound by the express terms of this Article to lay it before the Council.

The provisions as to time being duly observed, a delay of about nine months is secured. Ample opportunity is thus given for the people of each country concerned to insist on full information and explanation, and to weigh the consequences of resorting to war. If, after having had that opportunity, the final determination of any self-governing people is that war with all its known evils and unknown risk is more tolerable than any possible alternative, those who have to answer for such a determination will at any rate not be free to plead ignorance or surprise. If on the other hand either party, disregarding these provisions, attempted to gain a military advantage by sudden occupation of strategic points or of disputed territory, it would thereby put itself in the wrong and in a state of hostility with the whole League.

The section of the Commentary entitled "The Prevention of War" (pp. 209—215, below) should be carefully read as a whole with this and the next five Articles.

Article XIII.

The Members of the League agree that whenever any dispute shall arise between them which they recognise to be suitable for submission to arbitration and which cannot be satisfactorily settled by diplomacy, they will submit the whole subject-matter to arbitration.

Disputes as to the interpretation of a treaty, as to any question of international law, as to the existence of any fact which if established would constitute a breach of any international obligation, or as to the extent and nature of the reparation to be made for any such breach, are declared to be among those which are generally suitable for submission to arbitration.

For the consideration of any such dispute the court of arbitration to which the case is referred shall be the court agreed on by the parties to the dispute or stipulated in any convention existing between them.

The Members of the League agree that they will carry out in full good faith any award that may be rendered and that they will not resort to war against a Member of the League which complies therewith.   In the event of any failure to carry out such an award, the Council shall propose what steps should be taken to give effect thereto.

This Article lays down the principles on which "justiciable" controversies are to be dealt with.   It is fuller than the corresponding Article in the Draft; par. 2 is new, and handles a question which baffled the Peace Conference of 1907.

Under par. 1 how is it to be ascertained that a dispute "cannot be satisfactorily settled by diplomacy"? Are the parties themselves to be the judges of this fact, or if not, who? Does "satisfactorily" mean no more than "peaceably," or is it to be understood that a settlement is to be deemed satisfactory only when it is such as to give reasonable promise of being durable?

So far as the words go, there is room for a broad or for a narrow construction. But, having regard to the objects and general intention of the Covenant, and to the working of these provisions in practice, it appears that the wider view must be preferred. If the parties themselves say that they do not find ordinary diplomatic methods adequate to settle a dispute to their own satisfaction, it is hard to see who can be in a position to contradict them, or how it is possible to maintain that the dispute can be "satisfactorily settled by diplomacy." Certainly the Council will have no right (even if it were disposed) to make difficulties; it does not come into the procedure at all unless and until there is a failure to carry out an award. The result then is that arbitration is by no means confined to disputes that have reached an acute stage. As in civil affairs parties often agree, without any quarrel, to obtain judicial settlement of a doubtful question—it may be of boundaries, or of the distribution of public burdens, or of construing a standing contract, or of the devolution of property—by a friendly suit, as

we call it in English practice, so may any two Powers
refer any matter for arbitration which they think likely
to give trouble hereafter.   There are many questions of
a legal nature, boundary questions for instance, which
are better disposed of by a decision on the legal merits
than by diplomatic bargain and compromise.   It would
have saved a great expenditure of ink and some risk of
estrangement between Great Britain and the United States
if the Guiana boundary dispute between Great Britain
and Venezuela had been referred to the award of a judicial
commission, or of a third Power, forty or fifty years before
it suddenly became dangerous in 1895.   Only in those
days nobody thought of it.   The official tradition was
to let sleeping controversies lie in the hope that they might
finally perish in obscurity and never become known to
the general public: a tradition useful within bounds in
small affairs but hazardous in great ones.   On the whole
it is conceived that under this paragraph members of the
League may submit for arbitration, at their pleasure, any
matter in difference that is not manifestly trifling or incapable of judicial determination.

The second paragraph enumerates four classes of disputes as being "among those" that may generally be
considered justiciable.   Let it be well noted that the words
"among those" are expressly framed to exclude any inference that the list purports to be exhaustive.   There is
nothing to prevent other kinds of dispute from being submitted to arbitration if the parties desire it.   "Any question of international law" covers, of course, questions of
boundaries and territorial claims in so far as they are not

dependent on conventional obligations. We may say therefore for practical purposes that any question will be justiciable which the parties choose to make so, subject only to the condition of putting it in a form capable of a judicial answer.

Under the third paragraph the parties have full freedom to choose their own tribunal. All known methods of arbitration are open to them pending the establishment of the permanent court to be formed under the next Article, and indeed after it. Existing arbitration treaties, and references thereunder to the Hague tribunal, or to a standing special commission as the case may be (see p. 38, above), are in no way interfered with. It is hoped, no doubt, that ultimately the new permanent court will be preferred on its merits.

Par. 4 requires the parties to a submission to carry out the award, puts those who duly comply with it under the protection of the League, and makes it not only the right but the duty of the Council to see that failure to execute awards is not tolerated. The words " propose what steps should be taken to give effect thereto " are purposely elastic. The League might authorize the law-abiding party to execute the award itself, or it might take the matter into its own hands. It will be observed that the automatic sanctions of Article 16 do not apply to mere passive failure to perform an award, but this does not exclude the use of similar means of coercion under the present Article by special resolution of the League. Obstinate refusal to abide by an arbitral decision does not seem a likely event, for even in the absence of any international sanction obedience to awards made under treaties or special agreements was the rule, and the exceptions very few. Still the case of refusal or vexatious delay has to be provided for.

ARTICLE XIV.

The Council shall formulate and submit to the Members of the League for adoption plans for the establishment of, a Permanent Court of International Justice. The Court shall be competent to hear and determine any dispute of an international character which the parties thereto submit to it. The Court may also give an advisory opinion upon any, dispute or question referred to it by the Council or by the Assembly.

Here the founders of the League had to deal with a problem which has been the despair of publicists, official and unofficial, for several years. They have wisely chosen the only way to an effectual solution. Many problems of constructive reform are such that a body of delegates, expert or not expert, turned loose on it to discuss at large and free to discharge themselves even by a merely negative report will never agree, but a commission of competent persons who are not asked to report whether the thing can be done, but told that it has to be done, can and will do it. Now the Council is bound to prepare a scheme: no limit of time is assigned, and I do not think it would have been wise to prescribe one, but a reasonable time is to be understood: I should be disposed to estimate this at about a year from the Council getting to work. Materials are to hand in the debates of the Hague Conference of 1907, and the more rational of the plans more lately set forth by private enterprise. In the meantime, as we have already observed, all existing forms of arbitration are available. If anyone asks why they should not be accepted as sufficient, and the trouble of setting up a new court dispensed with, the Commentary supplies the answer.

" The Permanent Court of Justice . . . is essential for any real progress in international law. As things now stand, the political rather than the judicial aspect of the settlement of disputes is prominent in the Covenant, but ' political ' settlements can never be entirely satisfactory or just. Ultimately, and in the long run, the only alternative to war is law, and for the enthronement of law there is required such a continuous development of international jurisprudence, at present in its infancy, as can only be supplied by the progressive judgments of a Permanent Court working out its own traditions. Isolated instances of arbitration, however successful, can never result to the same extent in establishing the reign of law " (a).

It would be useless here to speculate on the manner in which the plan to be formulated is likely to secure fair representation on the court for the members of the League other than the principal Powers. Doubtless the Secretariat will prepare for the Council an analytical report on the schemes of selection and rotation already put forward at the Hague Conference and by sundry unofficial authors. A simpler way might be to let every State nominate a judge, with liberty for two or more to send in the same name, subject to a standard of qualification, and the

(a) See Appendix No. IV. for a fuller statement of reasons by the present writer published in April, 1919.

Assembly (excluding the representatives of those Powers who have a standing right to a seat in the court) choose the required number from that list by the proportional representation method of the transferable vote, now used in several countries for parliamentary and other elections and pretty generally understood. But the matter is now in the hands of the Council, who will have full command of expert advice, and there does not seem to be much room for volunteered suggestions.

The competence of the court extends to "any dispute of an international character which the parties thereto submit to it." One would think that any dispute between two sovereign States which they agree in thinking important enough to call for a judicial decision cannot well help being of an international character. Presumably the words are intended to quiet some doubt that was raised during the revision of the Covenant, for they do not appear in the Draft. In any case they are words of abundant caution which can do no harm, and enable the court to decline jurisdiction in the improbable event of attempts being made to abuse its process.

The power of the court to give an advisory opinion at the request of the Council or the Assembly has also been added in the final recension. It may well be found useful, and without an express declaration it would have been disputable whether the court could properly give effect to such a request. Nothing is said about the form of the proceeding, but it may be presumed that the court would sit in its usual manner and hear argument. There is European precedent in the statutory authority of the

Judicial Committee of the Privy Council to advise the
Crown on questions officially referred to it.   American
courts have held, I think uniformly so far as the occasion
has arisen, that it is beyond their competence, in the
absence of a special constitutional provision, to advise the
executive authorities of their respective jurisdictions.

ARTICLE XV.

If there should arise between Members of the League
any dispute likely to lead to a rupture, which is not submitted to arbitration as above, the Members of the League
agree that they will submit the matter to the Council.   Any
party to the dispute may effect such submission by giving
notice of the existence of the dispute to the Secretary-General,
who will make all necessary arrangements for a full investigation and consideration thereof.

For this purpose the parties to the dispute will communicate to the Secretary-General, as promptly as possible, statements of their case with all the relevant facts and papers,
and the Council may forthwith direct the publication thereof.

The Council shall endeavour to effect a settlement of the
dispute, and if such efforts are successful, a statement shall
be made public giving such facts and explanations regarding
the dispute and the terms of settlement thereof as the Council
may deem appropriate.

If the dispute is not thus settled, the Council, either unanimously or by a majority vote, shall make and publish a
report containing a statement of the facts of the dispute
and the recommendations which are deemed just and proper
in regard thereto.

Any Member of the League represented on the Council
may make public a statement of the facts of the dispute and
of its conclusions regarding the same.

If a report by the Council is unanimously agreed to by
the members thereof other than the Representatives of one
or more of the parties to the dispute, the Members of the
League agree that they will not go to war with any party
to the dispute which complies with the recommendations
of the report.

If the Council fails to reach a report which is unanimously
agreed to by the members thereof, other than the Repre-

sentatives of one or more of the parties to the dispute, the Members of the League reserve to themselves the right to take such action as they shall consider necessary for the maintenance of right and justice.

If the dispute between the parties is claimed by one of them, and is found by the Council to arise out of a matter which by international law is solely within the domestic jurisdiction of that party, the Council shall so report, and shall make no recommendation as to its settlement.

The Council may in any case under this Article refer the dispute to the Assembly. The dispute shall be so referred at the request of either party to the dispute, provided that such request be made within fourteen days after the submission of the dispute to the Council.

In any case referred to the Assembly, all the provisions of this Article and of Article XII. relating to the action and powers of the Council shall apply to the action and powers of the Assembly, provided that a report made by the Assembly, if concurred in by the Representatives of those Members of the League represented on the Council and of a majority of the other Members of the League, exclusive in each case of the Representatives of the parties to the dispute, shall have the same force as a report by the Council concurred in by all the members thereof other than the Representatives of one or more of the parties to the dispute.

We now come to the provisions for conciliation as distinct from judicial process.

Under this Article " a dispute referred to the Council can be dealt with by it in several ways:—

(1) " The Council can keep the matter in its own hands, as it is certain to do with any essentially political question in which a powerful State feels itself closely interested.

(2) " It can submit any dispute of a legal nature for the opinion of the Permanent Court, though in this case the finding of the Court will have no force till endorsed by the Council.

(3) "While keeping the matter in its own hands, the Council can refer single points for judicial opinion.

(4) "There is nothing to prevent the Council from referring any matter to a committee, or to prevent such a committee from being a standing body. An opening is left, therefore, for the reference of suitable issues to such non-political bodies as the 'commissions of conciliation' which are desired in many quarters. The reports of such committees would of course require the approval of the Council to give them authority, but the Covenant leaves wide room for development in this direction.

(5) "The Council may at any time refer a dispute to the Assembly. The procedure suggested under (2), (3) and (4) will then be open to the Assembly."

The text is fuller and more precise than its earlier form in the Draft. The fifth paragraph is new.

One could guess from the text alone that the work of the Council, or the Assembly under a reference from the Council, would in practice have to be done through committees, and that if cases of this kind were frequent they would come to be dealt with by a standing committee, so that in substance though not in form there would be a board or commission of conciliation such as is prominent in almost all recent schemes prior to the formation of the League. All doubt on this head is removed by the important explanation we have just quoted from the Commentary. Clearly the general intention is to give the widest possible scope for all and any forms of inquiry, discussion, and mediation that may be appropriate in the particular case. It was thought, seemingly, that a standing special council, however carefully chosen, would not have so much freedom of action as the Council of the League: also, perhaps, that experience alone can show whether there will be much or little occupation for any such body, and the creation of a special board, with the inevitable sub-departmental office and staff, would do no good at this stage and might do harm by weakening the Secretariat.

The security for publicity given by the third, fourth, and fifth paragraphs deserves particular attention. Without such provisions the lesser Powers might well stand in fear of compromises being made at their expense for reasons that would not bear the light of day. But these paragraphs make it impossible for any such things to be done in a corner. The liberty of publishing a separate report given by par. 5 is an additional safeguard. In practice the risk of such a report being published ought, at need, to be a sufficient inducement to the Council to state the facts adequately and fairly in its own report, and give due weight to the views of a minority or of any one considerable member.

Having regard to the variety of procedure purposely allowed by this Article, it was obviously neither practicable nor desirable to lay down a limit of time. In any case of real difficulty the more time can be gained the better.

ARTICLE XVI.

Should any Member of the League resort to war in disregard of its covenants under Articles XII., XIII., or XV., it shall *ipso facto* be deemed to have committed an act of war against all other Members of the League, which hereby undertake immediately to subject it to the severance of all trade or financial relations, the prohibition of all intercourse between their nationals and the nationals of the covenant-breaking State, and the prevention of all financial, commercial, or personal intercourse between the nationals of the covenant-breaking State and the nationals of any other State, whether a Member of the League or not.

It shall be the duty of the Council in such case to recommend to the several Governments concerned what effective military, naval or air force the Members of the League shall severally contribute to the armed forces to be used to protect the covenants of the League.

The Members of the League agree, further, that they will mutually support one another in the financial and economic measures which are taken under this Article, in order to minimise the loss and inconvenience resulting from the above measures, and that they will mutually support one another in resisting any special measures aimed at one of their number by the covenant-breaking State, and that they will take the necessary steps to afford passage through their territory to the forces of any of the Members of the League which are co-operating to protect the covenants of the League.

Any Member of the League which has violated any covenant of the League may be declared to be no longer a Member of the League by a vote of the Council concurred in by the Representatives of all the other Members of the League represented thereon.

The following are the breaches of covenant which are to put the wrongdoing State in a condition of hostility against all other members. Under Article 12, resort to war without submission to arbitration or inquiry, or, if the dispute is submitted, within three months after the award or report. Under Article 13, making war on a member of the League which complies with an award. Under Article 15, the like as to a member complying with the recommendations of a report made after inquiry by the Council or the Assembly.

It appears to be assumed that the occurrence and character of any such acts, if they do occur, will be notorious, and that the duty of the other members of the League to break off commercial relations with the offending member will arise at once without any direction from the Council. But as the Council is bound to take action under the second paragraph, it is clear that in practice it would issue a declaration within a very short time. " In the first instance, it is left to individual States to decide whether or not such a breach has occurred and an act of war against the League been thereby committed. To wait for the pronouncement of a court of justice or even of the Council would mean delay, and delay at this crisis might be fatal. Any State, therefore, is justified in such a case in breaking off relations with the offending State on its own initiative, but it is probable, in fact, that the smaller States, unless directly attacked, will wait to see what decision is taken by the Greater Powers or by the Council, which is bound to meet as soon as possible, and is certain to do so within a few hours."

The commercial sanction is not only automatic, but extends to a blockade cutting off trade even with subjects of States outside the League. Inasmuch as the offending State is to " be deemed to have committed an act of war against all other members of the League," it seems that this would be a war blockade and not a strengthened form

10 (2)

of the pacific blockade which was formerly disallowed by the majority of learned opinions, but nevertheless was established as part of modern international law by the practice of the nineteenth century. Thus a question would not arise which, so far as I know, has never been decided in any jurisdiction, namely, whether a pacific blockade is binding on third parties. It might have arisen during the pacific blockade of Crete in 1897. If a Dutch vessel had been captured by a British or French cruiser in an attempt to break that blockade, and the Dutch Government had asked by what right the Powers acting as the Concert of Europe claimed to forbid the subjects of States that were no parties to their proceedings to traffic with a Turkish port in time of peace, it is not easy to see what convincing answer could have been given in any terms recognized by the law of nations. At that time the present writer ventured to say to the ambassador of a Great Power in London (not now living) that the only sovereign whose position was correct from a strictly technical point of view was the Sultan of Turkey: from which that high diplomatic personage did not dissent. Of course a pacific blockade might always be treated as a hostile act and a cause of war by the government of the blockaded coast. Equally of course a pacific blockade was never declared except in cases where it was obviously not the interest of the government thus coerced to expose itself to severer measures. But this as well as various other minor problems may well be thought at this day to belong to a superseded order of international relations.

Any further steps of a warlike nature which may be

necessary to enforce the commercial blockade or suppress open resistance to the League are not automatic, but have to be provided for on the recommendation of the Council. Neither has that recommendation any compulsory authority. But any government requested to contribute to the common armed force will have had a voice in the Council; "each member from which a contribution is required has the right to attend the Council, with power of veto, during the consideration of its particular case." So says the Commentary, the right being apparently deduced from Art. 4, par. 5. Therefore the persuasive weight of the Council's recommendation should be as effectual as a command. It is assumed that the forces of the acting members will co-operate, see par. 3, but nothing is said about unity of plan or direction. Speaking with deference as a civilian, I do not see how the conditions necessary for prompt and decisive co-operation are to be fulfilled unless the League has already some organ in being, under whatever name, in the nature of a real general staff. The framers of the Commentary have not overlooked this difficulty, and meet it as follows:—

" But it is desirable at this point to meet the objection that under such conditions the League will always be late, and consequently offers no safeguard against sudden aggression.

" It is true that in default of a strong international striking force, ready for instant action in all parts of the world, the members of the League must make their own arrangements for immediate self-defence against any force that could be suddenly concentrated against them, relying on such understandings as they have come to with their neighbours previously for this purpose. There is nothing in the Covenant (see Article 21) to forbid defensive conventions between States,"—in fact France, Great Britain, and the United States have made such a convention (*b*)— " so long as they are really and solely defensive, and their contents are made public. They will, in fact, be welcomed, in so far as they tend to preserve the peace of the world.

" To meet the first shock of sudden aggression, therefore, States must rely on their own resistance and the aid of their neighbours. But where, as in the case of the moratorium being observed, the aggression is not sudden, it is certain that those Powers which suspect a breach of the Covenant will have consulted together unofficially to decide on precautionary measures and to concert plans to be immediately put into force if the breach of the Covenant takes place. In this event these meetings of the representatives of certain Powers will develop into the Supreme War Council of the League, advised by a joint staff. Some reasons why this staff must be an *ad hoc* body, and not a permanent one, have been stated under Article 8."

With all respect, I do not find this wholly satisfying.

There is a fairly well known form of carrying on enterprises undertaken not with a primary view to profit, but for public ends usually of an artistic sort, by means of a governing body whose members take on themselves to be guarantors to a limited extent. In this manner a reserve fund is provided by which the society can obtain credit for the expenses it has to incur and in the result, if all goes well, to cover out of the returns. It is well under-

(*b*) Ratified by France and Great Britain only down to the end of November, 1919.

stood that the guarantee is a last resource, and that an actual call on the guarantors would signify failure, or at least a grave emergency: nevertheless the known existence of the guarantee is a necessary condition of stability and confidence. It is not fanciful, in my judgment, to see here a real analogy to the sanctions of the League of Nations. We must hope that in practice threatening conditions will hardly ever be allowed to ripen to the point where even the penal suspension of commercial relations will have to be applied. But that can be accomplished only through the knowledge of all Powers concerned that the sanctions are there, and a well founded belief that at need they are ready to become effective. The more thoroughly the League is equipped for dealing with emergencies, the less likelihood will there be of coercive action being in fact required. Within the domestic jurisdiction of a well ordered State the peace is kept with little show of force because it is known to all men that whoever is rash enough to fall on the State's reserve power will be broken. Not that any government in the world can give perfect assurance against occasional and partial disturbance. Riots occur from time to time in every jurisdiction of any considerable extent. It is enough that men can go about their lawful business in peace at most times and in most places. So long as that is so, there is, in the current phrase of French eighteenth century writers, a *pays policé*. More cannot be expected of the League of Nations than is accomplished on the whole by the authorities of existing civilized commonwealths within their own bounds.

" The last paragraph of Article 16 is intended to meet

the case of a State which, after violating its covenants, attempts to retain its position on the Assembly and Council." No further comment appears to be called for.

A case not provided for in terms by this Article is that of unauthorized hostilities breaking out between two States in such circumstances that neither of them can be said to have made any honest endeavour for the preservation of peace, and so both of them are in fault. In such a case it seems obvious that whatever degree of penal sanction is needful ought to be applied impartially to both, and neither should be allowed to retain any advantage from its action. If anyone thinks the supposition extravagant, we beg to direct his attention to the lamentable current events in the eastern parts of Europe. Indeed, we may well think a reckless war of this kind between minor States less unlikely than a barefaced attack by a stronger Power on a weaker. Likely or not, we conceive that the event is covered in substance.

Several propounders of earlier schemes, both before and during the war, have pleaded for the abolition of national armaments and the formation of a cosmopolitan world police under the immediate control of an international authority. The founders of the League have not taken any notice of this proposal: they appear therefore to be clearly of opinion that (supposing it ultimately desirable) it is not practicable in our time, and those who are bold enough to maintain that this opinion is wrong may be left to make what they can of their own. Obviously the derogation from national sovereignty would go far beyond anything contemplated by the Covenant. If that objec-

tion were out of the way, there would still be extreme
difficulty in making a composite army, not to speak of a
navy, homogeneous and efficient (c), and in framing such
provisions for its control as would avoid the undue preponderance of a few Great Powers without running into
the absurdities of divided or alternating command, whose
effects may be learnt from the Greek historians.   And
when all was done, and nothing left anywhere capable of
opposing this new instrument, we should for our pains
have something very like an international Prætorian
guard, ready to be captured by the ambition of some
future Napoleon and used as the foundation of a new
military despotism.   There might be worse themes for
an imaginative writer, but there is no serious reason for
dwelling farther on the topic here.

It may be suggested, however, that a small mixed guard
of honour at the headquarters of the League would be free
from objection and an appropriate symbolic ornament,
having the same kind of moral significance as the presence
in London of select Indian officers attached to the King's
person.   This would not entail any interference with
ordinary local jurisdiction, though it may be fit to be
considered hereafter whether an extra-territorial character
should be accorded to the offices and precincts in the
occupation of the League.   In that event there would be
much less risk of friction than in the relations between the
Vatican and the Italian executive authorities in Rome,
which in fact have given no trouble for many years.

(c) The experience of the late Austro-Hungarian dual
monarchy may be taken as a warning.

Article XVII.

In the event of a dispute between a Member of the League and a State which is not a Member of the League, or between States not Members of the League, the State or States not Members of the League shall be invited to accept the obligations of membership in the League for the purposes of such dispute, upon such conditions as the Council may deem just.   If such invitation is accepted, the provisions of Articles XII. to XVI. inclusive shall be applied with such modifications as may be deemed necessary by the Council.

Upon such invitation being given the Council shall immediately institute an inquiry into the circumstances of the dispute and recommend such action as may seem best and most effectual in the circumstances.

If a State so invited shall refuse to accept the obligations of membership in the League for the purposes of such dispute, and shall resort to war against a Member of the League, the provisions of Article XVI. shall be applicable as against the State taking such action.

If both parties to the dispute when so invited refuse to accept the obligations of membership in the League for the purposes of such dispute, the Council may take such measures and make such recommendations as will prevent hostilities and will result in the settlement of the dispute.

" Article 17 asserts the claim of the League that no State, whether a member of the League or not, has the right to disturb the peace of the world till peaceful methods of settlement have been tried.   As in early English law any act of violence, wherever committed, came to be regarded as a breach of the King's peace,"—originally a privilege extended from the King's household and immediate surroundings, to persons in his service and places taken under his special protection—" so any and every sudden act of war is henceforward a breach of the peace of the League, which will exact due reparation."

In other words the League hereby gives notice that it

will act as the general guardian of public peace. This cannot impose any conventional obligation upon Powers that are not parties to the treaties embodying the Covenant; it is, like the Monroe doctrine, a declaration of policy and not an offer to be accepted or discussed. At the same time it is a material addition to the inducements to come into the League. For the rest, it is not expected that any considerable State will ultimately remain outside, so this Article is really in the nature of a transitory provision.

The Commentary points to the growth of the King's peace in England as a precedent for the new-born cosmopolitan peace of the League. This is no far-fetched academic illustration; the parallel is not only justified by historical fact, but closer than it appears at first sight, notwithstanding the want in the old European system (for the Holy Roman Empire was a futile pretence) of any central power that can be said to answer to the King's authority in England. Some such work as was done here in the King's name from the consolidation of the English provincial kingdoms to the great constructive work of the thirteenth century was done in modern Europe, in a clumsier but still analogous fashion, by the undefined concert of the Great Powers of which we have spoken in the introductory chapters. Here the King's protection was gradually extended for the security of traffic on the great highways, which accordingly were called the King's, and the protection of royal officers, permanent or temporary, however far away from the Court; and his jurisdiction, starting from offences against his own person and within

his own household, came to include under the head of
" Pleas of the Crown," as modern lawyers know it, all
serious crimes and ultimately all breaches of public law.
The so-called Concert of Europe had no such definite
starting point. But it did establish a certain number of
partial guarantees of independence and neutrality, regulations for European waterways and so forth, under a real
though imperfect conventional sanction; and these may
well be likened to the state of the nascent King's peace in
England. At this day the law of nations has arrived at
the point where a fearless constructive effort is called for,
on a greater scale than that which was happily undertaken
here under Edward I., but essentially of the same kind.

Moreover the parallel is not without its lessons in the
matters of police and armaments. The League of
Nations is making a King's peace. But the King's peace
demands a sheriff and the power of the county, as indeed,
to use terms that may better come home to a modern
American, the authority of the Supreme Court demands
a United States marshal. If we could call up Henry of
Bratton to peruse our Covenant, one of his first questions
would certainly be: Where is your sheriff? And if we
could summon Alexander Hamilton, he would no less
surely ask: Where is your United States marshal? I have
already ventured to express my opinion that the French
delegation to the Conference of Paris had a clearer vision
of the proper answer to those questions than their colleagues have yet attained.

Then as to armaments, he would indeed have been a
rash counsellor who should have advised Edward I. (if

we can conceive such rashness as possible) to suppress the feudal levies and armed retinues of his great lords in order that the King's peace might be firm. In the fulness of time that had to come, but the work was reserved for the Tudor kings and their servants. Any attempt in that direction in the thirteenth century would have provoked a rebellion capable of wrecking not only the King's peace but the kingdom. William the Conqueror had already, with great wisdom, required the direct allegiance of all men, from the highest to the lowest, but he never talked or dreamt of taking over immediate command. The only practicable course was to enlist and use existing means of defence and order on the side of royal authority, so far as might be. So it is at this day with the League of Nations. It may be that national armies will be needless a century or two hence; we must leave posterity to look to it.

There are people, and I suppose there always will be, who have no sense of history and no belief in its present use: just as there are some, not foolish otherwise, who can never learn the points of the compass or remember their bearings even in familiar places. In such people's eyes all these comparisons will be the merest antiquarian futility. Yet they do not despise recent precedent and tradition in their own affairs, or even think bills of exchange obsolete because they are a medieval invention. The so-called practical man who puts his trust in rule of thumb fails to see that ancient or medieval history is sometimes nearer to our affairs than what we call modern. Forms, institutions, manners, governments and the scale

and instruments of their action, have all changed greatly
since Roman legionaries marched on Roman roads in
Britain, and the rate of change has been increasing (notwithstanding the apparent stability which deceived many
but not all able men in the eighteenth century) ever since
the Reformation.   But the human nature of which all
these things are the trappings, and of which rulers and
legislators have to take account at their peril, has changed
very little.   If our best men make fewer and less dangerous
mistakes than the best of their ancestors, it is not that they
are better or wiser men in themselves, but that they have
more past experience to guide them, and ampler and more
exact means of knowledge.

Another sort of teachers err and will continue to err not
as men walking on earth in a fog, but as creatures cut
adrift from earth and soaring aloft in a cloud.   Ignorance
of anything but mankind is not their fault; they may be
very well informed.   Still less is want of faith to be laid
to their charge.   They despise history and its lessons
because they believe in some project for making a new
heaven and a new earth all at once, either their own or
some prophet's whom they acknowledge as their master,
and think all the world's troubles can be cured by the
mechanical removal, as it were, of this and that peccant
element on which they can lay their finger.   For them
society is a machine, and the problem is only to locate
some grit that lurks in the working parts; an easier task,
no doubt, if that were all, than the detection and counter-
working of enemy forms of life within a living organism.
Their favourite piece of grit may be capitalism, or

churches, or alcohol, or indirect taxation, or competition, or officialism, or the very existence of law and government, which William Morris, no small man, and Tolstoy, a great one, took for their scapegoat in all seriousness. Men of the world point out that from the beginning of history many prophets have tried many short cuts, of which some have done nothing but harm and none unmixed good. But neither fact nor argument will shake the fanatic's confidence that the secret of the real short cut is his at last, and this time the world will be proved wrong. Obviously no categorical disproof can be produced against him. As I begin this sentence I really have no proof that the sun will not blow up before it is finished. But it is finished and the sun goes on shining, and I shall continue to act on the faith of the solar system justifying the Nautical Almanack for my time and a long time after. The greater and saner part of mankind will believe, in spite of all dogmatists, that experience is worth using, and the wider it can be both in space and in time the better.

Need we say that the founders of the League of Nations are not fanatics advertising a panacea? They know as well as any critic that they are fallible men working with imperfect instruments on more or less refractory matter. So far, indeed, as there has been any competent censure of the peace treaties or of the Covenant, the exceptions have mostly been taken not to anything alleged to be too much, but to various things alleged to be too little; not to excess of zeal, but to lack of courage and faith. There is said to be overmuch compromise and caution, too many concessions to the old European spirit of selfish ambition, too little infusion of the new spirit that is to exorcise it. As it is no part of our undertaking to weigh these criticisms, we can only say that any result arrived at by the composite work of men representing many different interests and opinions must be exposed to censure of this kind; that in many cases the objectors' reasons are likely to be plausible; but that in a large proportion of those cases full knowledge would probably show the actual conclusion to be the best or the most tolerable one attainable here and now. The framers of the Covenant, at any rate, have honestly done their best to profit by both old and recent experience, to seek out the most promising paths of improvement, and to advance in them as far as can be safely done at present.

CHAPTER VIII.

THE LEAGUE IN PEACE.

(Treaties, Mandates, Economic Co-operation, Amendments.)

ARTICLE XVIII.

Every treaty or international engagement entered into hereafter by any Member of the League, shall be forthwith registered with the Secretariat and shall as soon as possible be published by it. No such treaty or international engagement shall be binding until so registered.

" ARTICLES 18—21 describe the new conditions which must govern international agreements if friendship and mutual confidence between peoples are to prevail; the first three provide that all treaties shall be (1) public, (2) liable to reconsideration at the instance of the Assembly, and (3) consonant with the terms of the Covenant. These provisions are of the very first importance."

The Commentary further explains why registration is made the one positive condition for the validity of treaties. If their force dated only from publication an uncertain element of delay would be introduced. The express duty of the Secretariat to publish the text as soon as possible will suffice as a precaution against secrecy.

The provisions of this group of Articles agree in substance with those of the Draft, but the order and to some extent the wording are varied.

ARTICLE XIX.

The Assembly may from time to time advise the reconsideration by Members of the League of treaties which have become inapplicable and the consideration of international conditions whose continuance might endanger the peace of the world.

" Article 19 should be read together with Article 11," which authorizes every member of the League to call the attention of the Council or the Assembly to conditions appearing likely to endanger the peace.

The weakness of these Articles, taken separately or together, is that they do not provide for any systematic revision or consolidation of the law of nations. That is a work which ought to be taken in hand and for which only the League is competent. Revival of the Hague Conferences in their original form is out of the question. But there is nothing to prevent either the Assembly or the Council from appointing a special commission for this purpose under the very wide powers given by Articles 3 and 4. It should be a permanent commission meeting at stated periods and reporting to the Council. Assuming its reports to be approved by the Council or the Assembly, they would still have to be adopted by the several members of the League in order to become authoritative. We are still a long way from the method suggested by Mr. Taft in 1915, and approved by several other writers. This was to create a competent expert body, under whatever name, for the formulation of international law, and to lay its projects, when approved by the executive of the League, before the constituent governments after the manner of statutory Orders in Council in this country, that is, to take effect unless objection is notified within a certain time. Some publicists went so far as to think that the drafts thus put forward might safely be enacted by a three-fourths majority of States.

Unless the League is content to leave international law in its present formless condition (which may be described as a body of undefined general custom partly consolidated in conventions of various extent and authority received by more or less general usage), further provision will have to be made in this behalf by the addition of one or more Articles to the Covenant. It is not a matter to be dealt with in haste, and it may well be that in the long run we shall gain by waiting patiently for some years. Meanwhile it is rather amusing to look back to the sanguine expectations of well-meaning publicists who thirty or forty years ago were cheerfully talking of codifying the law of nations without having given any serious attention to the practical difficulties of the undertaking. One or two complete projects of fairly recent date are in print.

ARTICLE XX.

The Members of the League severally agree that this Covenant is accepted as abrogating all obligations or understandings *inter se* which are inconsistent with the terms thereof, and solemnly undertake that they will not hereafter enter into any engagements inconsistent with the terms thereof.

In case any Member of the League shall, before becoming a Member of the League, have undertaken any obligations inconsistent with the terms of this Covenant, it shall be the duty of such Member to take immediate steps to procure its release from such obligations.

11 (2)

A general clause of this kind was obviously desirable even if not strictly necessary.

The next following Article indicates in a general way what kinds of international engagements may be deemed consistent with the Covenant. In any case of doubt the proper course of the member or members concerned would be to refer the question to the Council.

ARTICLE XXI.

Nothing in this Covenant shall be deemed to affect the validity of international engagements such as treaties of arbitration or regional understandings like the Monroe Doctrine for securing the maintenance of peace.

Engagements consistent with the Covenant " would include special treaties for compulsory arbitration "—which is a clear case—"and military conventions that are genuinely defensive." Such a Convention has already been made in two identical treaties between France of the one part and Great Britain and the United States of the other parts (June 28, 1919) (a). It is expressly provided that the treaty must be submitted to the Council and recognized as an engagement which is consistent with the Covenant of the League.

As to the Monroe Doctrine the Commentary says that " at first a principle of American foreign policy, it has become an international understanding, and it is not illegitimate for the people of the United States to ask that the Covenant should recognise this fact." It is at least doubtful whether this could have been truly said before the war, for German and Austrian publicists always disliked the Monroe Doctrine, and often took occasion to

(a) Only the Franco-British Treaty is ratified so far.

speak of it in barely civil or less than civil terms. Elsewhere, too, there has been a good deal of misconception, and it may not be superfluous to recall the elementary facts. " The origin of the Monroe Doctrine is well known. It was proclaimed in 1823 "—not in a diplomatic communication, but in a Presidential message to the Congress of the United States—" to prevent America becoming a theatre for the intrigues of European absolutism." President Monroe stated in effect that two kinds of action would be regarded as unfriendly by the United States: the settlement of a new colony on American ground by any European Power, and interference by any European Power with the independence of any American commonwealth or its freedom to determine its own form of government (b). There has not been any later official formulation of the doctrine; on the one occasion when it was most applicable, that of Napoleon III.'s ill-advised attempt to force a monarchical government under an Austrian prince on Mexico, there was no mention of it by name in the protest of the United States, really in the nature of an ultimatum, which made an end of that plan. In fact the diplomatic utterances of the United States have uniformly avoided the use of any language that might give colour to the charge of pretending to lay down a new rule of international law. As between the United States and Great Britain the case is rather different, for the second and at this day more important branch of the doctrine arose out of a suggestion made by Canning of joint British

(b) His actual words will be found in the Appendix below, No. 5.

and American opposition to the Holy Alliance in the matter of the Spanish-American republics, and it seems to have been in great part because of the slowness of communication at that time that there was not a joint or identical manifesto.

It may be asked why, in the face of this Article, a certain section of American politicians professes to be still uneasy about the Monroe Doctrine. American colleagues can answer that question better than any English commentator, and, what is more, without reserve. We therefore leave it in their hands. It is allowable, however, to note the fear expressed by a presumably detached Irish critic that the aim of the anti-Treaty and anti-Covenant agitators in the Republican party is less to secure that the world shall be made safe for democracy than that America shall be made unsafe for the Democrats (c).

ARTICLE XXII.

To those colonies and territories which as a consequence of the late war have ceased to be under the sovereignty of the States which formerly governed them and which are inhabited by peoples not yet able to stand by themselves under the strenuous conditions of the modern world, there should be applied the principle that the well-being and development of such peoples form a sacred trust of civilisation and that securities for the performance of this trust should be embodied in this Covenant.

The best method of giving practical effect to this principle is that the tutelage of such peoples should be entrusted to advanced nations who by reason of their resources, their experience or their geographical position, can best undertake this responsibility, and who are willing to accept it, and that this tutelage should be exercised by them as Mandatories on behalf of the League.

(c) The Irish Statesman, Sept. 13th, 1919, at p. 281.

The character of the mandate must differ according to the stage of the development of the people, the geographical situation of the territory, its economic conditions and other similar circumstances.

Certain communities formerly belonging to the Turkish Empire have reached a stage of development where their existence as independent nations can be provisionally recognised subject to the rendering of administrative advice and assistance by a Mandatory until such time as they are able to stand alone. The wishes of these communities must be a principal consideration in the selection of the Mandatory.

Other peoples, especially those of Central Africa, are at such a stage that the Mandatory must be responsible for the administration of the territory under conditions which will guarantee freedom of conscience or religion, subject only to the maintenance of public order and morals, the prohibition of abuses such as the slave trade, the arms traffic and the liquor traffic, and the prevention of the establishment of fortifications or military and naval bases and of military training of the natives for other than police purposes and the defence of territory, and will also secure equal opportunities for the trade and commerce of other Members of the League.

There are territories, such as South-West Africa and certain of the South Pacific Islands, which, owing to the sparseness of their population, or their small size, or their remoteness from the centres of civilisation, or their geographical contiguity to the territory of the Mandatory, and other circumstances, can be best administered under the laws of the Mandatory as integral portions of its territory, subject to the safeguards above mentioned in the interests of the indigenous population.

In every case of mandate, the Mandatory shall render to the Council an annual report in reference to the territory committed to its charge.

The degree of authority, control, or administration to be exercised by the Mandatory shall, if not previously agreed upon by the Members of the League, be explicitly defined in each case by the Council.

A permanent Commission shall be constituted to receive and examine the annual reports of the Mandatories and to advise the Council on all matters relating to the observance of the mandates.

This Article creates a sphere of activity for the League extending far beyond anything that was contemplated in earlier projects. European troubles will have to be quieted before it can come into full operation, but the Parliament of the South African Union has already accepted a mandate for the late German colony of South-West Africa.

Little is to be found in earlier publications on the subject that bears on the importance of the League's administrative work in time of peace. Gen. Smuts pointed to it, in advance though not much in advance of the Paris Conference, in words that merit special citation (p. 8 of his pamphlet):

"An attempt will be made in this sketch to give an essential extension to the functions of the League; indeed to look upon the League from a very different point of view, to view it not only as a possible means for preventing future wars, but much more as a great organ of the ordinary peaceful life of civilisation, as the foundation of the new international system which will be erected on the ruins of this war, and as the starting point from which the peace arrangements . . . . It is not sufficient for the League to be merely a sort of *deus ex machina*, called in in very grave emergencies when the spectre of war appears; if it is to last, it must be much more. It must become part and parcel of the common international life of States, it must be an ever visible, living, working organ of the polity of civilisation. It must function so strongly in the ordinary peaceful intercourse of States that it becomes irresistible in their disputes; its peace activity must be the foundation and guarantee of its war power."

He went on to deal at some length, and much on the lines adopted in the Covenant, with the government and protection of populations not capable of self-government. I do not find any clear forecast of the still wider undertakings contemplated in Art. 23.

The official Commentary has very little to say here, for the sufficient reason that the causes and the intention of the novel institution are set forth in the text itself. Only the last three paragraphs of this unusually full Article are really operative enactments; the most important of these is the requirement of an annual report to the Council from every mandatory authority. We say authority, not State; the possibility of a mandate being exercised by a joint commission in the name of more than one Power does not appear to be excluded, although such an arrangement would be desirable and workable only in some very special case.

Some persons may fear that a mandatory State will be exposed to officious intermeddling on the part of the League. Any one who is acquainted with the relations between the Colonial Office and our Crown Colonies may be apt to think that the danger is the other way, and that one duty of the Secretary-General will be to prevent the annual reports and the advice of the commission charged to examine them from degenerating into a perfunctory routine. Unless the Secretariat of the League is very unlike all other official departments all over the world, its temptation will be to keep its papers in order with as little trouble as possible, not to ask inconvenient questions, and not to interfere until the necessity for interference is

urgent (*d*). "Avant tout on ne veut pas d'histoires," the
French say with a conciseness we cannot match. I know
of one case in which a long series of complaints, not very
clearly or skilfully formulated, led to a commission being
sent out to report on the administration of justice in a
small Crown Colony. When that commission came into
touch with the facts on the spot, it found the complaints
more than justified on all material points. Indeed there
was not too much time to save the colony from ruin.
Action was effective enough in that case when taken, for
the result was a clean sweep of the whole judicial establishment.   The intelligence department of the League
must see to it that things do not come to such a pass in
any of the territories put under mandates.

ARTICLE XXIII.

Subject to and in accordance with the provisions of international conventions existing or hereafter to be agreed upon,
the Members of the League—

(a) will endeavour to secure and maintain fair and humane
conditions of labour for men, women and children
both in their own countries and in all countries to
which their commercial and industrial relations extend, and for that purpose will establish and maintain the necessary international organisations;

(b) undertake to secure just treatment of the native inhabitants of territories under their control;

(c) will entrust the League with the general supervision
over the execution of agreements with regard to the
traffic in women and children, and the traffic in
opium and other dangerous drugs;

(*d*) This does not apply without qualification to the class known
as "spending departments"; but their peculiar activity does not
concern us here, and on the clerical side of even those departments the desire of complete formal accuracy too often comes
before practical utility.

(d) will entrust the League with the general supervision
of the trade in arms and ammunition with the
countries in which the control of this traffic is necessary in the common interest;
(e) will make provision to secure and maintain freedom
of communications and of transit and equitable
treatment for the commerce of all Members of the
League. In this connection, the special necessities
of the regions devastated during the war of 1914
—1918 shall be borne in mind;
(f) will endeavour to take steps in matters of international
concern for the prevention and control of disease.

Here we have an even wider extension of the League's
competence and activity than in the preceding Article.
It is believed to be due to Continental publicists, but we
have not been able to trace its origin. There is a roughly
similar but much less developed Article in the German
project which will be found in the Appendix.

The corresponding provisions of the Draft were less
full, but contained an agreement " to establish as part of
the organisation of the League a permanent Bureau of
Labour" which is not here, but is replaced by the more
elastic words " the necessary national organisations." A
single Bureau, it seems to be thought, would not suffice
for the objects of par. (a), much less for those of the
whole Article. The lines on which this Article, especially
par. (a), is to be worked out were to some extent disclosed
at the General Labour Conference held at Washington
in November, 1919, which was in close touch with the
League though not formally under its authority. Full
accounts are not yet accessible, but the results are known
to be considerable.

The great political importance of Articles 22 and 23,

in addition to the positive benefits to be expected from
their application, is that they make the nations of the
civilized world active partners in a large field of humane
undertakings unconnected with any immediate danger of
war. In its very birth the League has outgrown and dis-
carded the narrow conception of it as a merely negative
system of mutual insurance; and this without any derogation from the independence of the member States.
There is nothing in either of these Articles whereby an
unwilling Power can be compelled to undertake any
specific task which it finds repugnant or even inconvenient.
Intimate counsel and free co-operation are the methods
proposed. It would be foolish not to be prepared for
occasional disappointment. The leagued Powers are a
squadron limited to a speed at which they can keep company. But if the temper of sincere endeavour is maintained, and the due measure of patience and tact is not
wanting, there is no assignable end to the fruit of good
works which these Articles may bring forth.

Article XXIV.

There shall be placed under the direction of the League
all international bureaux already established by general
treaties if the parties to such treaties consent. All such
international bureaux and all commissions for the regulation of matters of international interest hereafter constituted
shall be placed under the direction of the League.

In all matters of international interest which are regulated
by general conventions but which are not placed under the
control of international bureaux or commissions, the Secretariat of the League shall, subject to the consent of the
Council and if desired by the parties, collect and distribute
all relevant information and shall render any other assistance
which may be necessary or desirable.

The Council may include as part of the expenses of the Secretariat the expenses of any bureau or commission which is placed under the direction of the League.

Something has been said above (p. 81) of the various international administrative and regulative bodies already organized and at work under a number of Conventions. All these will now be brought into touch under the common direction of the League. Here again the Secretariat has an ample field of occupation quite beyond and apart from the League's primary object of preventing war.

ARTICLE XXV.

The Members of the League agree to encourage and promote the establishment and co-operation of duly authorised voluntary national Red Cross organisations having as purposes the improvement of health, the prevention of disease and the mitigation of suffering throughout the world.

This is a profitable supplementary Article of which the effect is to enlist the medical profession throughout the world in aid of the League's efforts for the welfare of humanity. Specific comment on the methods of working it out is a matter for experts of that profession rather than for lawyers and publicists.

ARTICLE XXVI.

Amendments to this Covenant will take effect when ratified by the Members of the League whose Representatives compose the Council and by a majority of the Members of the League whose Representatives compose the Assembly.

No such amendment shall bind any Member of the League which signifies its dissent therefrom, but in that case it shall cease to be a Member of the League.

Under this Article amendments can be carried only by a majority of the members constituting the Assembly on the unanimous recommendation of the Powers represented

on the Council. This is ample security against haste or
surprise. Nevertheless it seems far from unlikely that
the Covenant, like the Constitution of the United States,
may be supplemented by a group of amendments before
it is many years old; after which, if the precedent holds,
a long period of stability may follow. We have indicated
points on which it might be strengthened with advantage,
and others will probably be disclosed. So far as the wording goes, it will be observed that an amendment might be
framed and enacted by direct negotiation among the constituent Powers without any formal meeting of the Council
or the Assembly, but it cannot be supposed that such will
be the practice. Presumably the intention is to make
it clear that the consent of the Powers represented at a
particular meeting of the Council, or a majority of those
represented at a particular meeting of the Assembly, would
not suffice.

The Draft required a three-fourths majority of the
Powers represented in the Assembly; this was thought on
revision to be an excess of caution, as the leading Powers
have to be unanimous.

ANNEX TO THE COVENANT.

1. ORIGINAL MEMBERS OF THE LEAGUE OF NATIONS.
SIGNATORIES OF THE TREATY OF PEACE (e).

United States of America.	British Empire.	China.
Belgium.	Canada.	Cuba.
Bolivia.	Australia.	Czecho-Slovakia.
Brazil.	South Africa.	Ecuador.
	New Zealand.	France.
	India.	

(e) Belgium, Brazil, the British Empire and Dominions,
France, Italy, Japan, Peru and Uruguay have ratified the Treaty.
Greece is waiting to ratify all the peace treaties together.

Greece.	Japan.	Portugal.
Guatemala.	Liberia.	Roumania.
Haiti.	Nicaragua.	Serbia.
Hedjaz.	Panama.	Siam.
Honduras.	Peru.	Uruguay.
Italy.	Poland.	

STATES INVITED TO ACCEDE TO THE COVENANT.

*Argentine	Netherlands.	*Spain.
Republic.	Norway.	Sweden.
*Chile.	*Paraguay.	Switzerland.
Colombia.	*Persia.	Venezuela.
Denmark.	Salvador.	

The States whose names are thus * marked have in substance joined the League. Their adhesion will be formally complete when the Treaty comes into force.

With regard to the rest their accession is understood to be, with few exceptions if any, subject only to the delay necessary for satisfying legislative and constitutional requirements.

———————

The nations of the world stand at the parting of the ways. Temporary delays notwithstanding, the States joined in this League and Covenant will soon dispose of a greater collective power of counsel, united action, persuasion, and in the last resort enforced control, than has ever yet been in the hands of mortal rulers. Will the people and the leaders rise to the height of their great endeavour, or will they suffer ambition, greed, and envy to drag them down and renew the bad old days of strife in even more ruinous forms? Will the wise men of the future say of the leaders in action, as Alfred Lyall's Indian ascetic said:

> Is it a god or a king that comes,
> Both are evil and both are strong?

Or will he deem them worthy of the blessing invoked by the Psalmist on the just king? " Specie tua et pulchritudine tua intende, prospere procede, et regna, propter veritatem, et mansuetudinem, et iustitiam: et deducet te mirabiliter dextera tua."

" Because of truth, meekness and righteousness." That is the spirit in which the League of Nations must go forward if it is to earn the blessing. A constant will for justice even to the unjust is the first thing needful; next, perseverance in well-doing; ability for planning and means for execution are not wanting. Good will and perseverance being assured, both actors and spectators in so great a matter will still have need of patience. If they are oppressed by the sight of the war-clouds still lowering over sundry regions, let them recall the words of a wise Englishman, John Selden: " Though we had peace, yet 'twill be a great while ere things be settled: though the wind lie, yet after a storm the sea will work a great while." And if they are cast down by the failure of the Covenant to satisfy the whole world at once, or to realize in a few months the completion of tasks that former generations did not find it possible even to begin, let them take heart from the saying of Colbert, a great French man of affairs: "Il ne faut jamais se mettre dans l'esprit que ce que l'on fait est parfait. Mais il faut toujours chercher à avancer pour approcher de la perfection, qu'on ne trouve jamais." All human endeavour is subject to disappointment; nevertheless, if honest and competent, it seldom wholly fails, and an undertaking of unexampled scope and unbounded opportunities deserves endeavour of the best.

APPENDIX I.

DRAFT AGREEMENT FOR A LEAGUE OF NATIONS.

Presented to the Plenary Inter-Allied Conference of February 14, 1919.

COVENANT.

Preamble.

In order to promote international co-operation and to secure international peace and security by the acceptance of obligations not to resort to war, by the prescription of open, just and honourable relations between nations, by the firm establishment of the understandings of international law as the actual rule of conduct among governments, and by the maintenance of justice and a scrupulous respect for all treaty obligations in the dealings of organised peoples with one another, the Powers signatory to this Covenant adopt this constitution of the League of Nations.

Article 1.

The action of the High Contracting Parties under the terms of this Covenant shall be effected through the instrumentality of meetings of a Body of Delegates representing the High Contracting Parties, of meetings at more frequent intervals of an Executive Council, and of a permanent international Secretariat to be established at the Seat of the League.

ARTICLE 2.

Meetings of the Body of Delegates shall be held at stated intervals and from time to time as occasion may require for the purpose of dealing with matters within the sphere of action of the League. Meetings of the Body of Delegates shall be held at the Seat of the League, or at such other place as may be found convenient, and shall consist of representatives of the High Contracting Parties. Each of the High Contracting Parties shall have one vote, but may have not more than three representatives.

ARTICLE 3.

The Executive Council shall consist of representatives of the United States of America, the British Empire, France, Italy, and Japan, together with representatives of four other States, members of the League. The selection of these four States shall be made by the Body of Delegates on such principles and in such manner as they think fit. Pending the appointment of these representatives of the other States, representatives of   shall be members of the Executive Council.

Meetings of the Council shall be held from time to time as occasion may require, and at least once a year at whatever place may be decided on, or failing any such decision, at the Seat of the League, and any matter within the sphere of action of the League or affecting the peace of the world may be dealt with at such meetings.

Invitations shall be sent to any Power to attend a meeting of the Council at which matters directly affecting its interests are to be discussed, and no decision taken at any meeting will be binding on such Power unless so invited.

ARTICLE 4.

All matters of procedure at meetings of the Body of Delegates or the Executive Council, including the appointment of committees, to investigate particular matters, shall be regulated by the Body of Delegates or the Executive Council, and may be decided by a majority of the States represented at the meeting.

The first meeting of the Body of Delegates and of the Executive Council shall be summoned by the President of the United States of America.

ARTICLE 5.

The permanent Secretariat of the League shall be established at   which shall constitute the Seat of the League. The Secretariat shall comprise such secretaries and staff as may be required, under the general direction and control of a Secretary-General of the League, who shall be chosen by the Executive Council; the Secretariat shall be appointed by the Secretary-General, subject to confirmation by the Executive Council.

The Secretary-General shall act in that capacity at all meetings of the Body of Delegates or of the Executive Council.

The expenses of the Secretariat shall be borne by the States members of the League in accordance with the apportionment of the expenses of the International Bureau of the Universal Postal Union.

ARTICLE 6.

Representatives of the High Contracting Parties and officials of the League when engaged on the business of the League shall enjoy diplomatic privileges and immunities, and the buildings occupied by the League or its officials or by representatives attending its meetings shall enjoy the benefits of extraterritoriality.

ARTICLE 7.

Admission to the League of States not signatories to the Covenant and not named in the Protocol hereto as States to be invited to adhere to the Covenant, requires the assent of

12 (2)

not less than two-thirds of the States represented in the
Body of Delegates, and shall be limited to fully self-governing countries, including Dominions and Colonies.

No State shall be admitted to the League unless it is able
to give effective guarantees of its sincere intention to observe
its international obligations, and unless it shall conform to
such principles as may be prescribed by the League in regard
to its naval and military forces and armaments.

ARTICLE 8.

The High Contracting Parties recognise the principle
that the maintenance of peace will require the reduction of
national armaments to the lowest point consistent with
national safety and the enforcement by common action of
international obligations, having special regard to the geographical situation and circumstances of each State; and
the Executive Council shall formulate plans for effecting
such reduction. The Executive Council shall also determine
for the consideration and action of the several Governments
what military equipment and armament is fair and reasonable in proportion to the scale of forces laid down in the
programme of disarmament; and these limits, when adopted,
shall not be exceeded without the permission of the Executive Council.

The High Contracting Parties agree that the manufacture
by private enterprise of munitions and implements of war
lends itself to grave objections, and direct the Executive
Council to advise how the evil effects attendant upon such
manufacture can be prevented, due regard being had to the
necessities of those countries which are not able to manufacture for themselves the munitions and implements of war
necessary for their safety.

The High Contracting Parties undertake in no way to
conceal from each other the condition of such of their industries as are capable of being adapted to warlike purposes
or the scale of their armaments, and agree that there shall

be full and frank interchange of information as to their military and naval programmes.

ARTICLE 9.

A permanent Commission shall be constituted to advise the League on the execution of the provisions of Article 8 and on military and naval questions generally.

ARTICLE 10.

The High Contracting Parties undertake to respect and preserve as against external aggression the territorial integrity and existing political independence of all States members of the League. In case of any such aggression or in case of any threat or danger of such aggression the Executive Council shall advise upon the means by which this obligation shall be fulfilled.

ARTICLE 11.

Any war or threat of war, whether immediately affecting any of the High Contracting Parties or not, is hereby declared a matter of concern to the League, and the High Contracting Parties reserve the right to take any action that may be deemed wise and effectual to safeguard the peace of nations.

It is hereby also declared and agreed to be the friendly right of each of the High Contracting Parties to draw the attention of the Body of Delegates or of the Executive Council to any circumstances affecting international intercourse which threaten to disturb international peace or the good understanding between nations upon which peace depends.

ARTICLE 12.

The High Contracting Parties agree that should disputes arise between them which cannot be adjusted by the ordinary processes of diplomacy, they will in no case resort to war without previously submitting the questions and matters involved either to arbitration or to inquiry by the Executive Council and until three months after the award by the arbitrators or a recommendation by the Executive Council; and that they will not even then resort to war as against a member of the League which complies with the award of the arbitrators or the recommendation of the Executive Council.

In any case under this article, the award of the arbitrators shall be made within a reasonable time, and the recommendation of the Executive Council shall be made within six months after the submission of the dispute.

ARTICLE 13.

The High Contracting Parties agree that whenever any dispute or difficulty shall arise between them which they recognise to be suitable for submission to arbitration and which cannot be satisfactorily settled by diplomacy, they will submit the whole subject matter to arbitration. For this purpose the Court of arbitration to which the case is referred shall be the Court agreed on by the parties or stipulated in any Convention existing between them. The High Contracting Parties agree that they will carry out in full good faith any award that may be rendered. In the event of any failure to carry out the award, the Executive Council shall propose what steps can best be taken to give effect thereto.

ARTICLE 14.

The Executive Council shall formulate plans for the establishment of a Permanent Court of International Justice and this Court shall, when established, be competent to hear and determine any matter which the parties recognise as suitable for submission to it for arbitration under the foregoing article.

ARTICLE 15.

If there should arise between States members of the League any dispute likely to lead to a rupture, which is

not submitted to arbitration as above, the High Contracting
Parties agree that they will refer the matter to the Executive Council; either party to the dispute may give notice
of the existence of the dispute to the Secretary-General,
who will make all necessary arrangements for a full investigation and consideration thereof. For this purpose
the parties agree to communicate to the Secretary-General,
as promptly as possible, statements of their case with all
the relevant facts and papers, and the Executive Council
may forthwith direct the publication thereof.

Where the efforts of the Council lead to the settlement
of the dispute, a statement shall be published indicating
the nature of the dispute and the terms of settlement,
together with such explanations as may be appropriate.
If the dispute has not been settled, a report by the Council
shall be published, setting forth with all necessary facts
and explanations the recommendation which the Council
think just and proper for the settlement of the dispute.
If the report is unanimously agreed to by the members of
the Council other than the parties to the dispute, the High
Contracting Parties agree that they will not go to war with
any party which complies with the recommendation and
that, if any party shall refuse so to comply, the Council
shall propose the measures necessary to give effect to the
recommendation. If no such unanimous report can be
made, it shall be the duty of the majority and the privilege
of the minority to issue statements indicating what they
believe to be the facts and containing the recommendations
which they consider to be just and proper.

The Executive Council may in any case under this article
refer the dispute to the Body of Delegates. The dispute
shall be so referred at the request of either party to the
dispute, provided that such request must be made within
fourteen days after the submission of the dispute. In any
case referred to the Body of Delegates all the provisions
of this article and of article 12 relating to the action and

powers of the Executive Council shall apply to the action and powers of the Body of Delegates.

ARTICLE 16.

Should any of the High Contracting Parties break or disregard its covenants under article 12, it shall thereby *ipso facto* be deemed to have committed an act of war against all the other members of the League, which hereby undertake immediately to subject it to the severance of all trade or financial relations, the prohibition of all intercourse between their nationals and the nationals of the covenant-breaking State, and the prevention of all financial, commercial, or personal intercourse between the nationals of the covenant-breaking State and the nationals of any other State, whether a member of the League or not.

It shall be the duty of the Executive Council in such case to recommend what effective military or naval force the members of the League shall severally contribute to the armed forces to be used to protect the covenants of the League.

The High Contracting Parties agree, further, that they will mutually support one another in the financial and economic measures which are taken under this article, in order to minimise the loss and inconvenience resulting from the above measures, and that they will mutually support one another in resisting any special measures aimed at one of their number by the covenant-breaking State, and that they will afford passage through their territory to the forces of any of the High Contracting Parties who are co-operating to protect the covenants of the League.

ARTICLE 17.

In the event of disputes between one State member of the League and another State which is not a member of the League, or between States not members of the League, the High Contracting Parties agree that the State or States

not members of the League shall be invited to accept the
obligations of membership in the League for the purposes
of such dispute, upon such conditions as the Executive Council may deem just, and upon acceptance of any such invitation, the above provisions shall be applied with such modifications as may be deemed necessary by the League.

Upon such invitation being given the Executive Council
shall immediately institute an inquiry into the circumstances
and merits of the dispute and recommend such action as
may seem best and most effectual in the circumstances.

In the event of a Power so invited refusing to accept the
obligations of membership in the League for the purposes
of such dispute, and taking any action against a State
member of the League which in the case of a State member
of the League would constitute a breach of article 12, the
provisions of article 16 shall be applicable as against the
State taking such action.

If both parties to the dispute when so invited refuse to
accept the obligations of membership in the League for the
purposes of such dispute, the Executive Council may take
such action and make such recommendations as will prevent hostilities and will result in the settlement of the
dispute.

ARTICLE 18.

The High Contracting Parties agree that the League shall
be entrusted with the general supervision of the trade in
arms and ammunition with the countries in which the control of this traffic is necessary in the common interest.

ARTICLE 19.

To those colonies and territories which as a consequence of
the late war have ceased to be under the sovereignty of the
States which formerly governed them and which are inhabited by peoples not yet able to stand by themselves under
the strenuous conditions of the modern world, there should
be applied the principle that the well-being and development
of such peoples form a sacred trust of civilisation and that

securities for the performance of this trust should be embodied in the constitution of the League.

The best method of giving practical effect to this principle is that the tutelage of such peoples should be entrusted to advanced nations who by reason of their resources, their experience or their geographical position, can best undertake this responsibility, and that this tutelage should be exercised by them as mandatories on behalf of the League.

The character of the mandate must differ according to the stage of the development of the people, the geographical situation of the territory, its economic conditions and other similar circumstances.

Certain communities formerly belonging to the Turkish Empire have reached a stage of development where their existence as independent nations can be provisionally recognised subject to the rendering of administrative advice and assistance by a mandatory Power until such time as they are able to stand alone. The wishes of these communities must be a principal consideration in the selection of the mandatory Power.

Other peoples, especially those of Central Africa, are at such a stage that the mandatory must be responsible for the administration of the territory subject to conditions which will guarantee freedom of conscience or religion, subject only to the maintenance of public order and morals, the prohibition of abuses such as the slave trade, the arms traffic and the liquor traffic, and the prevention of the establishment of fortifications or military and naval bases, and of military training of the natives for other than police purposes, and the defence of territory, and will also secure equal opportunities for the trade and commerce of other members of the League.

There are territories, such as South-West Africa and certain of the South Pacific Islands, which, owing to the sparseness of their population, or their small size, or their remoteness from the centres of civilisation, or their geographical contiguity to the mandatory State, and other circumstances, can be best administered under the laws of the mandatory

State as integral portions thereof, subject to the safeguards above-mentioned in the interests of the indigenous population.

In every case of mandate, the mandatory State shall render to the League an annual report in reference to the territory committed to its charge.

The degree of authority, control, or administration to be exercised by the mandatory State shall if not previously agreed upon by the High Contracting Parties in each case be explicitly defined by the Executive Council in a special Act or Charter.

The High Contracting Parties further agree to establish at the seat of the League a Mandatory Commission to receive and examine the annual reports of the Mandatory Powers, and to assist the League in ensuring the observance of the terms of all mandates.

ARTICLE 20.

The High Contracting Parties will endeavour to secure and maintain fair and humane conditions of labour for men, women, and children, both in their own countries and in all countries to which their commercial and industrial relations extend; and to that end agree to establish as part of the organisation of the League a permanent Bureau of Labour.

ARTICLE 21.

The High Contracting Parties agree that provision shall be made through the instrumentality of the League to secure and maintain freedom of transit and equitable treatment for the commerce of all States members of the League, having in mind, among other things, special arrangements with regard to the necessities of the regions devastated during the war of 1914-1918.

ARTICLE 22.

The High Contracting Parties agree to place under the control of the League all international bureaux already established by general treaties if the parties to such treaties consent. Furthermore, they agree that all such international bureaux to be constituted in future shall be placed under the control of the League.

ARTICLE 23.

The High Contracting Parties agree that every treaty or international engagement entered into hereafter by any State member of the League shall be forthwith registered with the Secretary-General, and as soon as possible published by him, and that no such treaty or international engagement shall be binding until so registered.

ARTICLE 24.

It shall be the right of the Body of Delegates from time to time to advise the reconsideration by States members of the League of treaties which have become inapplicable, and of international conditions, of which the continuance may endanger the peace of the world.

ARTICLE 25.

The High Contracting Parties severally agree that the present Covenant is accepted as abrogating all obligations *inter se* which are inconsistent with the terms thereof, and solemnly engage that they will not hereafter enter into any engagements inconsistent with the terms thereof.

In case any of the Powers signatory hereto or subsequently admitted to the League shall, before becoming a party to this Covenant, have undertaken any obligations which are inconsistent with the terms of this Covenant, it shall be the duty of such Power to take immediate steps to procure its release from such obligations.

ARTICLE 26.

Amendments to this Covenant will take effect when ratified by the States whose representatives compose the Executive Council and by three-fourths of the States whose representatives compose the Body of Delegates.

APPENDIX II.

------◆--

THE COVENANT OF THE LEAGUE OF NATIONS

WITH A COMMENTARY THEREON.

[*Note.*—The Covenant of the League of Nations forms Part I of the Draft Treaties of Peace presented to the Delegates of the German Empire at Versailles on May 7, and to those of Austria at Saint-Germain on June 2, 1919. It is provided that these Treaties shall come into force as soon as they have been ratified by Germany and Austria respectively, and by three of the Principal Allied and Associated Powers. The Principal Allied and Associated Powers comprise the United States of America, the British Empire, France, Italy and Japan.]

The High Contracting Parties, in order to promote international co-operation and to achieve international peace and security by the acceptance of obligations not to resort to war, by the prescription of open, just and honourable relations between nations, by the firm establishment of the understandings of international law as the actual rule of conduct among Governments, and by the maintenance of justice and a scrupulous respect for all treaty obligations in the dealings of organised peoples with one another, agree to this Covenant of the League of Nations.

ARTICLE I.

The original Members of the League shall be those of the Signatories which are named in the Annex to this Covenant

and also such of those other States named in the Annex as
shall accede without reservation to this Covenant.   Such
accession shall be effected by a Declaration deposited with the
Secretariat within two months of the coming into force of
the Covenant.   Notice thereof shall be sent to all other
Members of the League.

Any fully self-governing State, Dominion or Colony not
named in the Annex, may become a Member of the League
if its admission is agreed to by two-thirds of the Assembly,
provided that it shall give effective guarantees of its sincere
intention to observe its international obligations, and shall
accept such regulations as may be prescribed by the League
in regard to its military, naval and air forces and armaments.

Any Member of the League may, after two years' notice
of its intention so to do, withdraw from the League, provided
that all its international obligations and all its obligations
under this Covenant shall have been fulfilled at the time
of its withdrawal.

ARTICLE II.

The action of the League under this Covenant shall be
effected through the instrumentality of an Assembly and
of a Council, with a permanent Secretariat.

ARTICLE III.

The Assembly shall consist of Representatives of the
Members of the League.

The Assembly shall meet at stated intervals and from
time to time as occasion may require, at the Seat of the
League or at such other place as may be decided upon.

The Assembly may deal at its meetings with any matter
within the sphere of action of the League or affecting the
peace of the world.

At meetings of the Assembly each Member of the League
shall have one vote, and may have not more than three
Representatives.

Article IV.

The Council shall consist of Representatives of the Principal Allied and Associated Powers, together with Representatives of four other Members of the League. These four Members of the League shall be selected by the Assembly from time to time in its discretion. Until the appointment of the Representatives of the four Members of the League first selected by the Assembly, Representatives of Belgium, Brazil, Greece, and Spain shall be members of the Council.

With the approval of the majority of the Assembly, the Council may name additional Members of the League whose Representatives shall always be members of the Council; the Council with like approval may increase the number of Members of the League to be selected by the Assembly for representation on the Council. .

The Council shall meet from time to time as occasion may require, and at least once a year, at the Seat of the League, or at such other place as may be decided upon.

The Council may deal at its meetings with any matter within the sphere of action of the League or affecting the peace of the world.

Any Member of the League not represented on the Council shall be invited to send a Representative to sit as a member at any meeting of the Council during the consideration of matters specially affecting the interests of that Member of the League.

At meetings of the Council each Member of the League represented on the Council shall have one vote, and may have not more than one Representative.

Article V.

Except where otherwise expressly provided in this Covenant or by the terms of the present Treaty, decisions at any meeting of the Assembly or of the Council shall require the agreement of all the Members of the League represented at the meeting.

All matters of procedure at meetings of the Assembly or of the Council, including the appointment of committees to investigate particular matters, shall be regulated by the Assembly or by the Council, and may be decided by a majority of the Members of the League represented at the meeting.

The first meeting of the Assembly and the first meeting of the Council shall be summoned by the President of the United States of America.

ARTICLE VI.

The permanent Secretariat shall be established at the Seat of the League. The Secretariat shall comprise a Secretary-General and such secretaries and staff as may be required.

The first Secretary-General shall be the person named in the Annex; thereafter the Secretary-General shall be appointed by the Council with the approval of the majority of the Assembly.

The secretaries and staff of the Secretariat shall be appointed by the Secretary-General with the approval of the Council.

The Secretary-General shall act in that capacity at all meetings of the Assembly and of the Council.

The expenses of the Secretariat shall be borne by the Members of the League in accordance with the apportionment of the expenses of the International Bureau of the Universal Postal Union.

ARTICLE VII.

The Seat of the League is established at Geneva.

The Council may at any time decide that the Seat of the League shall be established elsewhere.

All positions under or in connection with the League, including the Secretariat, shall be open equally to men and women.

Representatives of the Members of the League and officials of the League when engaged on the business of the League shall enjoy diplomatic privileges and immunities.

The buildings and other property occupied by the League or its officials or by Representatives attending its meetings shall be inviolable.

ARTICLE VIII.

The Members of the League recognise that the maintenance of peace requires the reduction of national armaments to the lowest point consistent with national safety and the enforcement by common action of international obligations.

The Council, taking account of the geographical situation and circumstances of each State, shall formulate plans for such reduction for the consideration and action of the several Governments.

Such plans shall be subject to reconsideration and revision at least every ten years.

After these plans shall have been adopted by the several Governments, the limits of armaments therein fixed shall not be exceeded without the concurrence of the Council.

The Members of the League agree that the manufacture by private enterprise of munitions and implements of war is open to grave objections. The Council shall advise how the evil effects attendant upon such manufacture can be prevented, due regard being had to the necessities of those Members of the League which are not able to manufacture the munitions and implements of war necessary for their safety.

The Members of the League undertake to interchange full and frank information as to the scale of their armaments, their military, naval and air programmes and the condition of such of their industries as are adaptable to war-like purposes.

ARTICLE IX.

A permanent Commission shall be constituted to advise the Council on the execution of the provisions of Articles I and VIII, and on military, naval and air questions generally.

Article X.

The Members of the League undertake to respect and preserve as against external aggression the territorial integrity and existing political independence of all Members of the League. In case of any such aggression or in case of any threat or danger of such aggression the Council shall advise upon the means by which this obligation shall be fulfilled.

Article XI.

Any war or threat of war, whether immediately affecting any of the Members of the League or not, is hereby declared a matter of concern to the whole League, and the League shall take any action that may be deemed wise and effectual to safeguard the peace of nations. In case any such emergency should arise the Secretary-General shall on the request of any Member of the League forthwith summon a meeting of the Council.

It is also declared to be the friendly right of each Member of the League to bring to the attention of the Assembly or of the Council any circumstance whatever affecting international relations which threatens to disturb international peace or the good understanding between nations upon which peace depends.

Article XII.

The Members of the League agree that if there should arise between them any dispute likely to lead to a rupture, they will submit the matter either to arbitration or to inquiry by the Council, and they agree in no case to resort to war until three months after the award by the arbitrators or the report by the Council.

In any case under this Article the award of the arbitrators shall be made within a reasonable time, and the report of the Council shall be made within six months after the submission of the dispute.

ARTICLE XIII.

The Members of the League agree that whenever any dispute shall arise between them which they recognise to be suitable for submission to arbitration and which cannot be satisfactorily settled by diplomacy, they will submit the whole subject-matter to arbitration.

Disputes as to the interpretation of a treaty, as to any question of international law, as to the existence of any fact which if established would constitute a breach of any international obligation, or as to the extent and nature of the reparation to be made for any such breach, are declared to be among those which are generally suitable for submission to arbitration.

For the consideration of any such dispute the court of arbitration to which the case is referred shall be the court agreed on by the parties to the dispute or stipulated in any convention existing between them.

The Members of the League agree that they will carry out in full good faith any award that may be rendered and that they will not resort to war against a Member of the League which complies therewith. In the event of any failure to carry out such an award, the Council shall propose what steps should be taken to give effect thereto.

ARTICLE XIV.

The Council shall formulate and submit to the Members of the League for adoption plans for the establishment of a Permanent Court of International Justice. The Court shall be competent to hear and determine any dispute of an international character which the parties thereto submit to it. The Court may also give an advisory opinion upon any dispute or question referred to it by the Council or by the Assembly.

ARTICLE XV.

If there should arise between Members of the League any dispute likely to lead to a rupture, which is not submitted

13 (2)

to arbitration as above, the Members of the League agree that they will submit the matter to the Council. Any party to the dispute may effect such submission by giving notice of the existence of the dispute to the Secretary-General who will make all necessary arrangements for a full investigation and consideration thereof.

For this purpose the parties to the dispute will communicate to the Secretary-General, as promptly as possible, statements of their case with all the relevant facts and papers, and the Council may forthwith direct the publication thereof.

The Council shall endeavour to effect a settlement of the dispute, and if such efforts are successful, a statement shall be made public giving such facts and explanations regarding the dispute and the terms of settlement thereof as the Council may deem appropriate.

If the dispute is not thus settled, the Council, either unanimously or by a majority vote, shall make and publish a report containing a statement of the facts of the dispute and the recommendations which are deemed just and proper in regard thereto.

Any Member of the League represented on the Council may make public a statement of the facts of the dispute and of its conclusions regarding the same.

If a report by the Council is unanimously agreed to by the members thereof other than the Representatives of one or more of the parties to the dispute, the Members of the League agree that they will not go to war with any party to the dispute which complies with the recommendations of the report.

If the Council fails to reach a report which is unanimously agreed to by the members thereof, other than the Representatives of one or more of the parties to the dispute, the Members of the League reserve to themselves the right to take such action as they shall consider necessary for the maintenance of right and justice.

If the dispute between the parties is claimed by one of

them, and is found by the Council to arise out of a matter which by international law is solely within the domestic jurisdiction of that party, the Council shall so report, and shall make no recommendation as to its settlement.

The Council may in any case under this Article refer the dispute to the Assembly. The dispute shall be so referred at the request of either party to the dispute, provided that such request be made within fourteen days after the submission of the dispute to the Council.

In any case referred to the Assembly, all the provisions of this Article and of Article XII relating to the action and powers of the Council shall apply to the action and powers of the Assembly, provided that a report made by the Assembly, if concurred in by the Representatives of those Members of the League represented on the Council and of a majority of the other Members of the League, exclusive in each case of the Representatives of the parties to the dispute, shall have the same force as a report by the Council concurred in by all the members thereof other than the Representatives of one or more of the parties to the dispute.

ARTICLE XVI.

Should any Member of the League resort to war in disregard of its covenants under Articles XII, XIII, or XV, it shall *ipso facto* be deemed to have committed an act of war against all other Members of the League, which hereby undertake immediately to subject it to the severance of all trade or financial relations, the prohibition of all intercourse between their nationals and the nationals of the covenant-breaking State, and the prevention of all financial, commercial, or personal intercourse between the nationals of the covenant-breaking State and the nationals of any other State, whether a Member of the League or not.

It shall be the duty of the Council in such case to recommend to the several Governments concerned what effective military, naval or air force the Members of the League shall severally contribute to the armed forces to be used to protect the covenants of the League.

The Members of the League agree, further, that they will mutually support one another in the financial and economic measures which are taken under this article, in order to minimise the loss and inconvenience resulting from the above measures, and that they will mutually support one another in resisting any special measures aimed at one of their number by the covenant-breaking State, and that they will take the necessary steps to afford passage through their territory to the forces of any of the Members of the League which are co-operating to protect the covenants of the League.

Any member of the League which has violated any covenant of the League may be declared to be no longer a Member of the League by a vote of the Council concurred in by the Representatives of all the other Members of the League represented thereon.

ARTICLE XVII.

In the event of a dispute between a Member of the League and a State which is not a Member of the League, or between States not Members of the League, the State or States not Members of the League shall be invited to accept the obligations of membership in the League for the purposes of such dispute, upon such conditions as the Council may deem just. If such invitation is accepted, the provisions of Articles XII to XVI inclusive shall be applied with such modifications as may be deemed necessary by the Council.

Upon such invitation being given the Council shall immediately institute an inquiry into the circumstances of the dispute and recommend such action as may seem best and most effectual in the circumstances.

If a State so invited shall refuse to accept the obligations of membership in the League for the purposes of such dispute, and shall resort to war against a Member of the League, the provisions of Article XVI shall be applicable as against the State taking such action.

If both parties to the dispute when so invited refuse to accept the obligations of membership in the League for the purposes of such dispute, the Council may take such measures and make such recommendations as will prevent hostilities and will result in the settlement of the dispute.

ARTICLE XVIII.

Every treaty or international engagement entered into hereafter by any Member of the League shall be forthwith registered with the Secretariat and shall as soon as possible be published by it. No such treaty or international engagement shall be binding until so registered.

ARTICLE XIX.

The Assembly may from time to time advise the reconsideration by Members of the League of treaties which have become inapplicable and the consideration of international conditions whose continuance might endanger the peace of the world.

ARTICLE XX.

The Members of the League severally agree that this Covenant is accepted as abrogating all obligations or understandings *inter se* which are inconsistent with the terms thereof, and solemnly undertake that they will not hereafter enter into any engagements inconsistent with the terms thereof.

In case any Member of the League shall, before becoming a Member of the League, have undertaken any obligations inconsistent with the terms of this Covenant, it shall be the duty of such Member to take immediate steps to procure its release from such obligations.

ARTICLE XXI.

Nothing in this Covenant shall be deemed to affect the validity of international engagements such as treaties of arbitration or regional understandings like the Monroe Doctrine for securing the maintenance of peace.

ARTICLE XXII.

To those colonies and territories which as a consequence of the late war have ceased to be under the sovereignty of the States which formerly governed them and which are inhabited by peoples not yet able to stand by themselves under the strenuous conditions of the modern world, there should be applied the principle that the well-being and development of such peoples form a sacred trust of civilisation and that securities for the performance of this trust should be embodied in this Covenant.

The best method of giving practical effect to this principle is that the tutelage of such peoples should be entrusted to advanced nations who by reason of their resources, their experience or their geographical position, can best undertake this responsibility, and who are willing to accept it, and that this tutelage should be exercised by them as Mandatories on behalf of the League.

The character of the mandate must differ according to the stage of the development of the people, the geographical situation of the territory, its economic conditions and other similar circumstances.

Certain communities formerly belonging to the Turkish Empire have reached a stage of development where their existence as independent nations can be provisionally recognised subject to the rendering of administrative advice and assistance by a Mandatory until such time as they are able to stand alone. The wishes of these communities must be a principal consideration in the selection of the Mandatory.

Other peoples, especially those of Central Africa, are at such a stage that the Mandatory must be responsible for the administration of the territory under conditions which will guarantee freedom of conscience or religion, subject only to the maintenance of public order and morals, the prohibition of abuses such as the slave trade, the arms traffic and the liquor traffic, and the prevention of the establishment of fortifications or military and naval bases and of military training of the natives for other than police purposes and the defence of territory, and will also secure equal opportunities for the trade and commerce of other Members of the League.

There are territories, such as South-West Africa and certain of the South Pacific Islands, which, owing to the sparseness of their population, or their small size, or their remoteness from the centres of civilisation, or their geographical contiguity to the territory of the Mandatory, and other circumstances, can be best administered under the laws of the Mandatory as integral portions of its territory, subject to the safeguards above mentioned in the interests of the indigenous population.

In every case of mandate, the Mandatory shall render to the Council an annual report in reference to the territory committed to its charge.

The degree of authority, control, or administration to be exercised by the Mandatory shall, if not previously agreed upon by the Members of the League, be explicitly defined in each case by the Council.

A permanent Commission shall be constituted to receive and examine the annual reports of the Mandatories and to advise the Council on all matters relating to the observance of the mandates.

ARTICLE XXIII.

Subject to and in accordance with the provisions of international conventions existing or hereafter to be agreed upon, the Members of the League—

(a) will endeavour to secure and maintain fair and humane conditions of labour for men, women, and children, both in their own countries and in all countries to which their commercial and industrial relations extend, and for that purpose will establish and maintain the necessary international organisations;

(*b*) undertake to secure just treatment of the native inhabitants of territories under their control;

(*c*) will entrust the League with the general supervision over the execution of agreements with regard to the traffic in women and children, and the traffic in opium and other dangerous drugs;

(*d*) will entrust the League with the general supervision of the trade in arms and ammunition with the countries in which the control of this traffic is necessary in the common interest;

(*e*) will make provision to secure and maintain freedom of communications and of transit and equitable treatment for the commerce of all Members of the League. In this connection, the special necessities of the regions devastated during the war of 1914-1918 shall be borne in mind;

(*f*) will endeavour to take steps in matters of international concern for the prevention and control of disease.

Article XXIV.

There shall be placed under the direction of the League all international bureaux already established by general treaties if the parties to such treaties consent. All such international bureaux and all commissions for the regulation of matters of international interest hereafter constituted shall be placed under the direction of the League.

In all matters of international interest which are regulated by general conventions but which are not placed under the control of international bureaux or commissions, the Secretariat of the League shall, subject to the consent of the Council and if desired by the parties, collect and distribute all relevant information and shall render any other assistance which may be necessary or desirable.

The Council may include as part of the expenses of the Secretariat the expenses of any bureau or commission which is placed under the direction of the League.

Article XXV.

The Members of the League agree to encourage and pro-mote the establishment and co-operation of duly authorised voluntary national Red Cross organisations having as purposes the improvement of health, the prevention of disease and the mitigation of suffering throughout the world.

Article XXVI.

Amendments to this Covenant will take effect when ratified by the Members of the League whose Representatives compose the Council and by a majority of the Members of the League whose Representatives compose the Assembly.

No such amendment shall bind any Member of the League which signifies its dissent therefrom, but in that case it shall cease to be a Member of the League.

ANNEX TO THE COVENANT.

1. Original Members of the League of Nations.

Signatories of the Treaty of Peace.

United States of America.	Cuba.	Liberia.
Belgium.	Czecho-Slovakia.	Nicaragua.
Bolivia.	Ecuador.	Panama.
Brazil.	France.	Peru.
British Empire.	Greece.	Poland.
Canada.	Guatemala.	Portugal.
Australia.	Haiti.	Roumania.
South Africa.	Hedjaz.	Serb-Croat-Slovene
New Zealand.	Honduras.	State.
India.	Italy.	Siam.
China.	Japan.	Uruguay.

States Invited to Accede to the Covenant.

Argentine	Netherlands.	Spain.
Republic.	Norway.	Sweden.
Chile.	Paraguay.	Switzerland.
Colombia.	Persia.	Venezuela.
Denmark.	Salvador.	

2. FIRST SECRETARY-GENERAL OF THE LEAGUE OF NATIONS.
The Hon. Sir James Eric Drummond, K.C.M.G., C.B.

[*Outside:* For the present the enemy States (Germany, Austria, Hungary, Bulgaria, Turkey); Russia, Finland, future Baltic States, a few minor independent or semi-sovereign States.]

COMMENTARY ON THE LEAGUE OF NATIONS COVENANT.

The first draft of the Covenant of the League of Nations was published on February 14, 1919; in the weeks following its publication the League of Nations Commission had the benefit of an exchange of views with the representatives of thirteen neutral Governments, and also of much criticism on both sides of the Atlantic. The Covenant was subjected to careful re-examination, and a large number of amendments were adopted. In its revised form it was unanimously accepted by the Representatives of the Allied and Associated Powers in Plenary Conference at Paris on April 28, 1919.

The document that has emerged from these discussions is not the Constitution of a super-State, but, as its title explains, a solemn agreement between sovereign States, which consent to limit their complete freedom of action on certain points for the greater good of themselves and the world at large. Recognising that one generation cannot hope to bind its successors by written words, the Commission has worked throughout on the assumption that the League must continue to depend on the free consent, in the last resort, of its component States; this assumption is evident in nearly every article of the Covenant, of which the ultimate and most effective sanction must be the public opinion of the civilised world. If the nations of the future are in the main selfish, grasping and warlike, no instrument or machinery will restrain them. It is only possible to establish an organisation which may make peaceful co-operation easy and hence customary, and to trust in the influence of custom to mould opinion.

But while acceptance of the political facts of the present has been one of the principles on which the Commission has worked, it has sought to create a framework which should make possible and encourage an indefinite development in accordance with the ideas of the future. If it has been chary of prescribing what the League shall do, it has been no less chary of prescribing what it shall not do. A number of amendments laying down the methods by which the League should work, or the action it should take in certain events, and tending to greater precision generally, have been deliberately rejected, not because the Commission was not in sympathy with the proposals, but because it was thought better to leave the hands of the statesmen of the future as free as possible, and to allow the League, as a living organism, to discover its own best lines of development.

The Members of the League.

Article I contains the conditions governing admission to the League, and withdrawal from it. On the understanding that the Covenant is to form part of the Treaty of Peace, the article has been so worded as to enable the enemy Powers to agree to the constitution of the League, without at once becoming members of it. It is hoped that the original Members of the League will consist of the thirty-two Allied and Associated Powers signatories of the Treaty of Peace, and of thirteen neutral States.

It is to be noted that original Members must join without reservation, and must therefore all accept the same obligations.

The last paragraph is an important affirmation of the principle of national sovereignty, while providing that no State shall be able to withdraw simply in order to escape the consequences of having violated its engagements. It is believed that the concession of the right of withdrawal will, in fact, remove all likelihood of a wish for it, by freeing States from any sense of constraint, and so tending to their more whole-hearted acceptance of membership.

The Organs of the League.

Articles II—VII describe the constitutional organs of the League.

The Assembly, which will consist of the official representatives of all the Members of the League, including the British Dominions and India, is the Conference of States provided for in nearly all schemes of international organisation, whether or not these also include a body of popular representatives. It is left to the several States to decide how their respective delegations shall be composed; the members need not all be spokesmen of their Governments.

The Assembly is competent to discuss all matters concerning the League, and it is presumably through the Assembly that the assent of the Governments of the world will be given to alterations and improvements in international law (see Article XIX), and to the many conventions that will be required for joint international action.

Its special functions include the selection of the four minor Powers to be temporarily represented on the Council, the approval of the appointment of the Secretary-General, and the admission (by a two-thirds majority) of new members.

Decisions of the Assembly, except in certain specified cases, must be unanimous. At the present stage of national feeling, sovereign States will not consent to be bound by legisla-

tion voted by a majority, even an overwhelming majority, of
their fellows. But if their sovereignty is respected in theory,
it is unlikely that they will permanently withstand a strong
consensus of opinion, except in matters which they consider vital.

The Assembly is the supreme organ of the League of
Nations, but a body of nearly 150 members, whose decisions
require the unanimous consent of some 50 States, is plainly
not a practical one for the ordinary purposes of international
co-operation, and still less for dealing with emergencies.
A much smaller body is required, and, if it is to exercise real
authority, it must be one which represents the actual distribution of the organised political power of the world.

Such a body is found in the Council, the central organ of
the League, and a political instrument endowed with greater
authority than any the world has hitherto seen. In form its
decisions are only recommendations, but when those who
recommend include the political chiefs of all the Great
Powers and of four other Powers selected by the States of
the world in assembly, their unanimous recommendations are
likely to be irresistible.

The mere fact that these national leaders, in touch with
the political situation in their respective countries, are to
meet once a year, at least, in personal contact for an exchange
of views, is a real advance of immense importance in international relations. Moreover, there is nothing in the
Covenant to prevent their places being taken, in the intervals
between the regular meetings, by representatives permanently resident at the Seat of the League, who would
tend to create a common point of view, and could consult and
act together in an emergency. The pressure of important
matters requiring decision is likely to make some such permanent body necessary, for the next few years at least.

The fact that for the decisions of the Council, as of the
Assembly, unanimity is ordinarily required, is not likely to
be a serious obstacle in practice. Granted the desire to agree,

which the conception of the League demands, it is believed that agreement will be reached, or at least that the minority will acquiesce. There would be little practical advantage, and a good deal of danger, in allowing the majority of the Council to vote down one of the Great Powers. An important exception to the rule of unanimity is made by the clause in Article XV providing that, in the case of disputes submitted to the Council, the consent of the parties is not required to make its recommendations valid.

The second paragraph of Article IV allows for the admission of Germany and Russia to the Council when they have established themselves as Great Powers that can be trusted to honour their obligations, and may also encourage small Powers to federate or otherwise group themselves for joint permanent representation on the Council. Provision is made for securing that such increase in the permanent membership of the Council shall not swamp the representatives of the small Powers, but no fixed proportion between the numbers of the Powers in each category is laid down.

The interests of the small Powers are further safeguarded by the fifth paragraph of Article IV. Seeing that decisions of the Council must be unanimous, the right to sit " as a member " gives the State concerned a right of veto in all matters specially interesting it, except in the settlement of disputes to which it is a party. The objection that this provision will paralyse the efforts of the Council does not seem valid, as it is most unlikely that the veto would be exercised except in extremely vital matters.

The relations between the Assembly and the Council are purposely left undefined, as it is held undesirable to limit the competence of either. Cases will arise when a meeting of the Assembly would be inconvenient, and the Council should not therefore be bound to wait on its approval. Apart from the probability that the representatives of States on the Council will also sit in the Assembly, a link between the two bodies is supplied by the Permanent Secretariat, or new international Civil Service.

This organisation has immense possibilities of usefulness, and a very wide field will be open for the energy and initiative of the first Secretary-General. One of the most important of his duties will be the collection, sifting, and distribution of information from all parts of the world. A reliable supply of facts and statistics will in itself be a powerful aid to peace. Nor can the value be exaggerated of the continuous collaboration of experts and officials in matters tending to emphasise the unity, rather than the diversity of national interests.

The Prevention of War.

Articles VIII—XVII, forming the central and principal portion of the Covenant, contain the provisions designed to secure international confidence and the avoidance of war, and the obligations which the members of the League accept to this end. They comprise:—

(1.) Limitation of armaments.

(2.) A mutual guarantee of territory and independence.

(3.) An admission that any circumstance which threatens international peace is an international interest.

(4.) An agreement not to go to war till a peaceful settlement of a dispute has been tried.

(5.) Machinery for securing a peaceful settlement, with provision for publicity.

(6.) The sanctions to be employed to punish a breach of the agreement in (4).

(7.) Similar provisions for settling disputes where States not members of the League are concerned.

All these provisions are new, and together they mark an enormously important advance in international relations.

Article VIII makes plain that there is to be no dictation by the Council or anyone else as to the size of national forces. The Council is merely to formulate plans, which the Governments are free to accept or reject. Once accepted, the members agree not to exceed them. The formulation and acceptance of such plans may be expected to take shape in a general Disarmament Convention, supplementary to the Covenant.

The interchange of information stipulated for in the last paragraph of the Article will, no doubt, be effected through the Commission mentioned in Article IX. The suggestion that this Commission might be given a general power of inspection and supervision, in order to ensure the observance of Article VIII, was rejected for several reasons. In the first place, such a power would not be tolerated by many national States at the present day, but would cause friction and hostility to the idea of the League; nor, in fact, is it in harmony with the assumption of mutual good faith on which the League is founded, seeing that the members agree to exchange full and frank information; nor, finally, would it really be of practical use. Preparations for war on a large scale cannot be concealed, while no inspection could hope to discover such really important secrets as new gases and explosives and other inventions of detail. The experience of our own Factory Acts shows what an army of officials is required to make inspection efficient, and how much may escape observation even then. In any case, the League would certainly receive no better information on such points of detail from a Commission than that obtained through their ordinary intelligence services by the several States.

Nor can the Commission fill the rôle of an International General Staff. The function of a General Staff is preparation for war, and the latter requires the envisagement of a definite enemy. It would plainly be impossible for British officers to take part in concerting plans, however hypothetical, against their own country, with any semblance of reality; and all the members of a staff must work together with complete confidence. It is further evident that no State would communicate to the nationals of its potential enemies the information as to its own strategic plans necessary for a concerted scheme of defence. The most that can be done in this direction by the Commission is to collect non-confidential information of military value, and possibly to work out certain transit questions of a special character.

In *Article* X the word "external" shows that the League cannot be used as a Holy Alliance to suppress national or other movements within the boundaries of the Member States, but only to prevent forcible annexation from without.

It is important that this article should be read with *Articles* XI and XIX, which make it plain that the Covenant is not intended to stamp the new territorial settlement as sacred and unalterable for all time, but, on the contrary, to provide machinery for the progressive regulation of international affairs in accordance with the needs of the future. The absence of such machinery, and the consequent survival of treaties long after they had become out of date, led to many of the quarrels of the past; so that these articles may be said to inaugurate a new international order, which should eliminate, so far as possible, one of the principal causes of war.

Articles XII—XVI contain the machinery for the peaceful settlement of disputes, and the requisite obligations and sanctions, the whole hinging on the cardinal agreement that a State which goes to war without submitting its ground of quarrel to arbitrators or to the Council, or without waiting till three months after the award of the former or the recommendation of the latter, or which goes to war in defiance of such award or recommendation (if the latter is agreed to by all members of the Council not parties to the dispute), thereby commits an act of war against all the other members of the League, which will immediately break off all relations with it and resort, if necessary, to armed force.

The result is that private war is only contemplated as possible in cases when the Council fails to make a unanimous report, or when (the dispute having been referred to the Assembly) there is lacking the requisite agreement between all the Members of the Council and a majority of the other States. In the event of a State failing to carry out the terms of an arbitral award, without actually resorting to war, it is left to the Council to consider what steps should be taken to give effect to the award; no such provision is made in the case of failure to carry out a unanimous recommendation by the Council, but it may be presumed that the latter would bring pressure of some kind to bear.

In this, as in other cases, not the least important part of the pressure will be supplied by the publicity stipulated for in the procedure of settlement. The obscure issues from which international quarrels arise will be dragged out into the light of day, and the creation of an informed public opinion made possible.

Article XIII, while not admitting the principle of compulsory arbitration in any class of disputes, to some extent recognises the distinction evolved in recent years between justiciable and non-justiciable causes, by declaring that in certain large classes of disputes recourse to arbitration is *prima facie* desirable.

The permanent Court of Justice, to be set up under *Article* XIV, is essential for any real progress in international law. As things now stand, the political rather than the judicial aspect of the settlement of disputes is prominent in the Covenant, but " political " settlements can never be entirely satisfactory or just. Ultimately, and in the long run, the only alternative to war is law, and for the enthronement of law there is required such a continuous development of international jurisprudence, at present in its infancy, as can only be supplied by the progressive judgments of a Permanent Court working out its own traditions. Isolated instances of arbitration, however successful, can never result to the same extent in establishing the reign of law.

Under *Article* XV a dispute referred to the Council can be dealt with by it in several ways:—

(1) The Council can keep the matter in its own hands, as it is certain to do with any essentially political question in which a powerful State feels itself closely interested.

(2) It can submit any dispute of a legal nature for the opinion of the Permanent Court, though in this case the finding of the Court will have no force till endorsed by the Council.

(3) While keeping the matter in its own hands, the Council can refer single points for judicial opinion.

(4) There is nothing to prevent the Council from referring any matter to a committee, or to prevent such a committee from being a standing body. An opening is left, therefore, for the reference of suitable issues to such non-political bodies as the " Commissions of Conciliation " which are desired in many quarters. The reports of such committees would of course require the approval of the Council to give them authority, but the Covenant leaves wide room for development in this direction.

(5) The Council may at any time refer a dispute to the Assembly. The procedure suggested under (2) (3) and (4) will then be open to the Assembly.

It has been already pointed out that, in the settlement of disputes under this article, the consent of the parties themselves is not necessary to give validity to the recommendations of the Council. This important provision removes any inconvenience that might arise in this connection from the right (see Article IV) of every Power to sit as member of the Council during the discussion of matters specially affecting it. We may expect that any Power claiming this right in the case of a dispute will be given the option of declaring itself a party to the dispute or not. If it declares itself a party, it will lose its right of veto; if not, it will be taken to disinterest itself in the question, and will not be entitled to sit on the Council.

The sanctions of *Article* XVI, with the exception of the last paragraph, apply only to breaches of the Covenant involving a resort to war. In the first instance, it is left to individual States to decide whether or not such a breach has occurred and an act of war against the League been thereby committed. To wait for pronouncement of a Court of Justice or even of the Council would mean delay, and delay at this crisis might be fatal. Any State, therefore, is justified in such a case in breaking off relations with the offending State on its own initiative, but it is probable, in fact, that the smaller States, unless directly attacked, will wait to see what decision is taken by the Great Powers or by the Council, which is bound to meet as soon as possible, and is certain to do so within a few hours. It is the duty of the Council, with the help of its military, naval and air advisers, to recommend what effective force each Member of the League shall supply; for this purpose, each Member from which a contribution is required has the right to attend the Council, with power of veto, during the consideration of its particular case. The several contingents will therefore be settled by agreement, as is indeed necessary if the spirit of the Covenant is to be preserved, and if joint action is to be efficacious. But it is desirable at this point to meet the objection that under such conditions the League will always be late, and consequently offers no safeguard against sudden aggression.

It is true that, in default of a strong international striking force, ready for instant action in all parts of the world, the Members of the League must make their own arrangements for immediate self-defence against any force that could be suddenly concentrated against them, relying on such understandings as they have come to with their neighbours previously for this purpose. There is nothing in the Covenant (see Article XXI) to forbid defensive conventions between States, so long as they are really and solely defensive, and their contents are made public. They will, in fact, be welcomed, in so far as they tend to preserve the peace of the world.

To meet the first shock of sudden aggression, therefore, States must rely on their own resistance and the aid of their neighbours. But where, as in the case of the moratorium being observed, the aggression is not sudden, it is certain that those Powers which suspect a breach of the Covenant will have consulted together unofficially to decide on precautionary measures and to concert plans to be immediately put into force if the breach of the Covenant takes place. In this event these meetings of the representatives of certain Powers will develop into the Supreme War Council of the League, advised by a joint staff. Some reasons why this staff must be an *ad hoc* body, and not a permanent one, have been stated under Article VIII.

The last paragraph of Article XVI is intended to meet the case of a State which, after violating its covenants, attempts to retain its position on the Assembly and Council.

Article XVII asserts the claim of the League that no State, whether a member of the League or not, has the right to disturb the peace of the world till peaceful methods of settlement have been tried. As in early English law any act of violence, wherever committed, came to be regarded as a breach of the King's peace, so any and every sudden act of war is henceforward a breach of the peace of the League, which will exact due reparation.

Treaties and Understandings.

Articles XVIII—XXI describe the new conditions which must govern international agreements if friendship and mutual confidence between peoples are to prevail; the first three provide that all treaties shall be (1) public, (2) liable to reconsideration at the instance of the Assembly, and (3) consonant with the terms of the Covenant. These provisions are of the very first importance.

Article XVIII makes registration, and not publication, the condition for the validity of treaties, for practical reasons, since experience shows that the number of new international agreements continually being made is likely to be so great that instant publication may not be possible; but it is the duty of the Secretariat to publish all treaties as soon as this can be done.

Article XIX should be read together with Article XI.

Article XXI makes it clear that the Covenant is not intended to abrogate or weaken any other agreements, so long as they are consistent with its own terms, into which the members of the League may have entered, or may enter hereafter, for the further assurance of peace. Such agreements would include special treaties for compulsory arbitration, and military conventions that are genuinely defensive. The Monroe doctrine and similar understandings are put in the same category. They have shown themselves in history to be not instruments of national ambition, but guarantees of peace.

The origin of the Monroe doctrine is well known. It was proclaimed in 1823 to prevent America becoming a theatre for the intrigues of European absolutism. At first a principle of American foreign policy, it has become an international understanding, and it is not illegitimate for the people of the United States to ask that the Covenant should recognise this fact. In its essence it is consistent with the spirit of the Covenant, and indeed the principles of the League, as expressed in Article X, represent the extension to the whole world of the principles of the doctrine; while, should any dispute as to the meaning of the latter ever arise between American and European Powers, the League is there to settle it.

The Functions of the League in Peace.

Articles XXII—XXV cover the greater part of the ordinary peace-time activities of the League.

Article XXII introduces the principle, with reference to the late German colonies and territories of the Ottoman Empire, that countries as yet incapable of standing alone should be administered for the benefit of the inhabitants by selected States, in the name, and on behalf, of the League, the latter exercising a general supervision. The safeguards which enlightened public opinion demands will in each case be inserted in the text of the actual convention conferring the Mandate. No provision is made in the Covenant for the extension of such safeguards to the other similar dependencies of the Members of the League, but it may be hoped that the maintenance of a high standard of administration in the mandate territories will react favourably wherever a lower standard now exists, and the mandatory principle may prove to be capable of wide application.

The saving clause at the beginning of *Article* XXIII makes it clear that the undertakings following do not bind the members of the League further than they are bound by existing or future conventions supplementary to the Covenant.

Undertaking (*a*) throws the ægis of the League over the Labour Convention, which itself provides that membership of the League shall carry with it membership of the new permanent Labour organisation; (*b*) applies to territories not covered by Article XXII; (*d*) refers to the arms traffic with uncivilised and semi-civilised countries. The matters specially mentioned in this article are to be taken merely as instances of the many questions in which the League is interested. Conventions relating to some of these, such as Freedom of Transit and Ports, Waterways and Railways, are now being prepared; with regard to a large number of others similar conventions may be expected in the future.

Article XXIV is of great importance, as it enlarges the sphere of usefulness of the Secretariat of the League to an indefinite degree. The Covenant has laid the foundations on which the statesmen and peoples of the future may build up a vast structure of peaceful international co-operation.

Amendment of the Covenant.

The provisions of *Article* XXVI facilitate the adoption of amendments to the Covenant, seeing that all ordinary decisions of the Assembly have to be unanimous.

The second paragraph was inserted to meet the difficulties of certain States which might fail to secure the assent of their proper constitutional authorities to an amendment agreed to by the Council and the majority of the Assembly. They are now given the option of accepting the amendment or withdrawing from the League; but there is little doubt that, if the League becomes an institution of real value, the choice will be made in favour of accepting proposals that already command such wide assent.

It is the facility of amendment ensured by this article, and the absence of restrictions on the activities of the Assembly, the Council and the Secretariat, which make the constitution of the League flexible and elastic, and go far to compensate for the omissions and defects from which no instrument can be free that represents the fusion of so many and various currents of thought and interest.

APPENDIX III.

——◆——

THE GERMAN SCHEME FOR A LEAGUE OF NATIONS.

————

[From "The New Europe," May 15, 22, 1919. The original is reproduced in "The League of Nations," Berne, May 3, from the "Deutsche Allgemeine Zeitung," April 24, *sub tit.* "Gesetzentwurf der Deutschen Regierung für die Errichtung eines Völkerbundes vom 23 April 1919." Articles 38, 39 throw an interesting side-light on the German conception of the State's relation to the Press. Art. 43 shows the nature of German pious wishes after the war. As a whole the scheme is much more formal and elaborate than the Covenant.]

————

I.—FUNDAMENTAL PRINCIPLES.

1. The League of Nations shall, by means of compulsory arbitration in international disputes without resort to force of arms, lay the foundation of lasting peace between its members upon the moral force of right, and shall serve the spiritual and material progress of humanity by way of international co-operation. The League shall be permanent and shall constitute a united body for common defence against external aggression. The members shall guarantee one another's territorial integrity, and shall refrain from interference in each other's domestic affairs.

2. The especial objects of the League of Nations are:—

(a) Prevention of international disputes.

(b) Disarmament.

(c) Assurance of free commercial relations and of general economic equality.

(d) Protection of national minorities.

(e) Creation of an international labour charter.

(f) Regulation of colonial matters.

(g) Co-ordination of existing and future international institutions.

(h) Creation of a World Parliament.

3. The League of Nations shall comprise:—

(a) All belligerent States, including those which have arisen during the war.

(b) All neutral States which were formerly connected with The Hague Arbitration League.

(c) All other States admitted by consent of two-thirds of the existing members of the League. Membership of the League of Nations shall be open to the Papacy.

4. The members pledge themselves to conclude no private treaty which is variance with the objects of the League, and to enter into no secret engagements whatever. Any such existing treaties shall be dissolved.

Secret treaties shall be null and void.

II.—CONSTITUTION.

5. The organs of the League of Nations shall be:—

(a) The Congress of States.

(b) The World Parliament.

(c) The permanent International Tribunal.

(d) The International Board of Mediation.

(e) The International Administrative Boards.

(f) The Chancellery.

A. *The Congress of States.*

6. The Congress of States shall be the assembly of the representatives of the League of Nations. Each State shall have from one to three representatives; the representatives of each State may only vote unanimously.

7. The Congress shall meet at least once in every three years.

8. The Congress shall conduct the business of the League of Nations in so far as it is not delegated to other bodies; the Congress shall elect at its first meeting a standing Committee, which shall conduct business in the intervals between the meetings of the Congress.

9. The decisions of the Congress, in so far as is not otherwise provided by the treaty, shall be made by a majority of two-thirds of the States represented. Otherwise the Congress shall itself determine its procedure.

B. *The World Parliament.*

10. The first World Parliament shall be composed of representatives of the several Parliaments of the States belonging to the League. Each individual Parliament shall elect one delegate for every million inhabitants of the State it represents; but no Parliament may send more than ten representatives.

11. The future composition of the World Parliament shall be determined by the World Parliament itself, with the assent of the Congress of States.

12. The sanction of the World Parliament shall be requisite for:—

· (a) Alteration in the constitution of the League.

(b) The establishment of generally valid international legal standards.

(c) The appointment of new officials of the League.

(d) The determination of the budget of the League.

In these matters the World Parliament shall also have the right of initiative.

13. The World Parliament shall meet simultaneously with the Congress of States. Otherwise it shall regulate its own procedure.

C. *The Permanent International Tribunal.*

14. The International Tribunal shall be elected by the Congress of States for a period of nine years, in the following manner:—

Each State shall propose at least one and not more than four persons, who are fit and ready to assume the office of judge.

One at least of the nominees shall not be a subject of the nominating State.

Each State shall name fifteen persons out of the list of nominees; the fifteen persons who receive the highest number of votes shall be elected judges. When judges vacate their posts their places shall be taken by those persons who received the next highest number of votes, in the order of the number of votes received.

15. The decisions of the Tribunal shall be given by a bench of three members, of whom each party shall elect one. In case the parties do not agree in their choice of chairman, the chairman shall be nominated by the Tribunal in plenary session.

D. *The International Board of Mediation.*

16. Each State shall nominate for the International Board of Mediation four electors in whom it has confidence. The electors shall meet together and elect by a majority of votes the fifteen members of the Board of Mediation, as well as ten substitutes, whose order of succession shall be determined in the election.

17. The decisions of the Board of Mediation shall be given by a bench of five members, of whom each party shall select two. In case the parties fail to agree in their choice of a chairman, the chairman shall be nominated by the Board of Mediation in plenary session.

18. The members of the Board of Mediation may neither be in the active service of the State to which they belong

nor may they be simultaneously members of any other body
of the League of Nations.

They shall reside at the seat of the League of Nations.

E. *The International Administrative Boards.*

19. The League of Nations shall promote all efforts towards the co-ordination of the common interests of the
nations, and shall work for the extension of existing and
the creation of new international institutions. This applies
especially to the spheres of law, economics, and finance.

20. Unions already in existence shall as far as possible
be affiliated to the League of Nations.

21. All international bureaux already instituted by collective treaties shall, if the contracting parties consent, be
placed under the supervision of the League.

22. All international bureaux which shall be instituted
in future shall be under the supervision of the League.

F. *The Chancellery of the League.*

23. The officials of the Chancellery shall be nominated
by the Standing Committee of the Congress of States, and be
under its supervision.

24. The Chancellery shall be the common bureau of all
the organs of the League of Nations. Its procedure shall
be determined by the Standing Committee of the Congress of
States.

25. The Chancellery shall publish all decisions and an-
nouncements of the organs of the League of Nations in its
official gazette. The members of the League of Nations
shall pledge themselves to publish the decisions and an-
nouncements of the Congress of States and of the International Board of Mediation in their official publications in
the original text and in the language of the country and to
submit them to their legislative bodies.

26. The members of the League of Nations shall pledge
themselves to hand in to the Chancellery for publication

in the official gazette of the League all international treaties which they conclude.

G. *Position of the League Officials.*

27. All members of the International Boards and of the World Parliament, with the exception of those who are themselves subjects of the State in which the League is domiciled, shall enjoy the usual diplomatic privileges in that State.

28. The members of the World Parliament shall enjoy in the State of which they are subject the same rights as members of Parliament in that State.

III.—PEACEFUL ARBITRATION IN INTERNATIONAL DISPUTES.

29. All international disputes which have proved incapable of settlement by diplomatic means and for the settlement of which no private court of arbitration has been agreed upon, must be settled either by the permanent International Tribunal or by the International Board of Mediation.

30. The regular organ for the settlement of international legal disputes shall be the International Tribunal. Each member of the League of Nations has a right to institute an action in this court, which must be answered by the opposing party. The verdicts shall be given in the name of the League of Nations. The same applies to the procedure of the Board of Mediation.

31. Besides disputes between States, the International Tribunal is competent to deal with—

(a) Actions brought by private persons against foreign States and heads of States, if the State courts have declared themselves incompetent.

(b) Disputes between the subjects of the various States which are members of the League of Nations, in so far as the disputes concern the interpretation of State treaties.

32. The right to conclude arbitration treaties in the case of individual disputes or certain kinds of dispute is reserved

to the States concerned; on the other hand, they shall not have this power if it is a question of the interpretation of general and written standards of international law or the interpretation of the statute of the League of Nations.

33. If, in an international dispute before the International Tribunal, the defendant objects that it is a question of a pure conflict of interests, or of a legal case of predominantly political significance, the Tribunal shall deal first with this objection. If it finds the objection justified it shall transfer the dispute to the Board of Mediation for settlement.

If the dispute is brought before the Board of Mediation, and the objection is there raised that the matter under consideration is a purely legal one, the Board of Mediation shall refer the case in the first instance to the International Tribunal, which shall decide whether the dispute is to be referred back or whether it shall remain to be tried before the Tribunal.

34. The Tribunal shall draft a scheme of procedure on the basis of the Hague Agreement concerning the peaceable settlement of international disputes of 18 October, 1907; this scheme shall require the assent of the Congress of States in order to become effective. The method of procedure before the Board of Mediation shall be determined by the Board itself.

Both the Tribunal and the Board of Mediation shall be empowered to regulate the dispute for the duration of the proceedings by a temporary enactment.

35. The decision of the Tribunal shall ensue in accordance with the international agreements, with international customary law, and with the general principles of law and equity.

36. The decisions of the Tribunal or of the Board of Mediation shall oblige the State in question to execute [their] tenor honourably and loyally.

P. **15**

IV.—PREVENTION OF INTERNATIONAL DISPUTES.

37. If the Board of Mediation ascertains that tension has arisen in the relations between individual States of the League it may offer its mediation to the States concerned. These States shall then be obliged to discuss the matter before the Board of Mediation, and to provide it with the materials for a proposal for the solution of the question.

38. Each member of the League shall be bound to combat insulting treatment of another State, whether verbally, in writing, or in pictorial representation, by legislative and administrative means. If this obligation is violated, the injured State may appeal to the decision of the International Tribunal.

39. A mutual obligation shall exist between the States of the League to rectify on every occasion such actual assertions as may have been published by the press of one State to the prejudice of another. If this rectification is declined the International Tribunal shall decide.

V.—DISARMAMENT.

40. The members of the League shall so limit their armaments on land and in the air as to maintain only the forces required to ensure the safety of their country. They shall limit their armaments on sea to the forces necessary for the protection of their coasts.

41. The estimate of the total yearly expenditure on armaments, and the balance sheet, as well as the figures of the effective forces in troops and war material of all kinds, especially warships, shall be handed in every year to the Chancellery of the League and be published by the Chancellery in the official gazette of the League of Nations.

42. For the carrying out of disarmament a special agreement shall be made, which shall also comprehend international control over the observance of the agreements made.

The agreement shall form an essential part of the constitution of the League of Nations.

43. Sea supremacy shall be entrusted to the League of Nations. The League shall exercise this supremacy through an international marine police force, the organisation of which shall be determined by special agreement.

The forces necessary for the marine police shall be apportioned between the maritime States of the League of Nations by the agreement.

No armed ships except the ships of the marine police force shall be permitted upon the sea.

44. The straits and canals indispensable for international sea traffic shall be open to the ships of all members of the League on equal terms.

45. No State belonging to the League of Nations may treat the sea and inland shipping of another State of the League less favourably than its own or than that of the most-favoured country. This shall apply especially to the enjoyment of coaling and loading facilities. Coastal shipping shall be regulated by special agreement. As regards the seaworthiness of the ships and the conditions on board, the laws of the State under whose flag the ship sails shall be recognised as authoritative, pending regulation by the League of Nations.

46. The air shall be free to the flying machines of all States belonging to the League, without distinction. To carry out this principle a special agreement shall be made which shall regulate, among other matters, forced landings on the territory of the State traversed, and the guaranteeing of the Customs dues.

47. No State belonging to the League of Nations shall be restricted in the free use of cable and wireless communication.

48. The legal position of the subjects of one State of the League in the territory of another, in regard to personal liberty, religious freedom, and the rights of residence and of settlement, as well as legal protection, shall be regulated

15 (2)

by, a special agreement, on the basis of the greatest possible equality with the native inhabitants.

49. In carrying on trade, industry and agriculture, the subjects of one State of the League shall be on an equal footing with the natives in another State of the League, especially in respect of the taxes and charges involved.

50. The States belonging to the League shall neither directly nor indirectly participate in measures which aim at the continuation or resumption of the economic war. The right of taking coercive measures shall be reserved to the League of Nations.

51. Goods of all kinds travelling to or from the territory of a State of the League shall be free of all transit duty in the territories of the States belonging to the League.

52. Reciprocal trade within the League of Nations shall not be hampered by prohibitions on import, export or transit, except in so far as this may be necessary for reasons of public health and quarantine regulations, or for the carrying out of internal economic legislation.

53. The individual States belonging to the League shall be free to regulate their economic relations with one another, taking into consideration the special requirements, by separate agreements in other matters as well as in the relations above mentioned.

They shall recognise as the object of their efforts the creation of a universal commercial treaty.

VII.—PROTECTION OF NATIONAL MINORITIES.

54. National minorities within the individual States of the League shall be guaranteed a national life of their own, especially in respect of language, education, church, art, science and press.

The carrying out of this principle shall be determined by special agreement, which shall lay down in particular the manner in which the right of minorities shall be asserted before the organs of the League of Nations.

VIII.—LABOUR LAW.

55. One of the chief tasks of the League shall be to assure to the working classes of all member States an existence worthy of human beings and pleasure in their work. For this purpose a special agreement, appended as a supplement, shall regulate for the workers the questions of freedom of movement, right of coalition, equality as between natives and foreigners in respect of conditions of work, labour arbitration, State insurance, protection of labour, conditions of home labour, supervision of labour, and the international realisation and development of these standards.

56. For the supervision and extension of the labour code there shall be instituted a Universal Labour Department in the Chancellery of the League.

IX.—COLONIES.

57. For the administration of those colonies which are not self-governing the League of Nations shall create an international system in the following spheres:—

(a) Protection of natives against slavery, alcohol, traffic in arms and munitions, epidemics, forced labour and forcible expropriation.

(b) Provision for the health, education, and well-being of the natives and assurance of their freedom of conscience.

(c) Ensurement of peace by neutralisation of colonial territories and prohibition of militarisation.

58. Freedom of religious practices and of missionary work in all the colonies shall be guaranteed to the religious communities recognised in the States belonging to the League.

59. Freedom of economic activity shall be guaranteed to the subjects of all the States of the League in every colony, regard being had to the general provisions regarding freedom of traffic above enunciated.

60. For the carrying out and supervision of the above provisions a Universal Colonial Office shall be set up. Commissioners of the League of Nations shall be bound in every colony to superintend the observance of the above provisions.

61. The fate of territories of a colonial character, not directly or indirectly attached to the League of Nations, can be settled only by the decision of the League in favour of one of its members.

X.—EXECUTION OF DECISIONS.

62. If a State belonging to the League shall refuse to carry out the verdicts, decisions or orders of a competent organ of the League, or if it shall violate any other provision of the Constitution of the League, the Board of Mediation shall in plenary session of fifteen members decide upon the application of coercive measures.

63. These measures may in particular consist in:—

(a) The breaking off of diplomatic relations by all the other States;

(b) Restriction or breaking off of economic relations, especially prohibition of imports and exports, differential customs treatment, stoppage of passenger and goods traffic and of news, and seizure of vessels;

(c) Military measures, entrusted to the injured State alone or in conjunction with other States.

64. Each State shall have the right, in case of attack on its territory, not only to resort to the legal resources of the League, but to immediate self-defence.

65. All costs and damages incurred by the States belonging to the League, either singly or in common, resulting from the employment of these measures, shall be borne by the State breaking the peace.

XI.—EXPENSES.

66. The total expenses of the League of Nations shall be defrayed by the States of the League according to an accountancy system which shall be determined by the Congress of States modelled on the system adopted by the World Postal Union.

APPENDIX IV.

----◆----

THE WORK OF THE LEAGUE OF NATIONS:
The International Civil Court.

[This short article by the present writer is reprinted from the " Law Quarterly Review " of April, 1919, as a practically contemporary and independent statement of the same reasons, in substance, as are given by the official Commentary for the establishment of a permanent judicial Court.]

While publicists are still discussing the possibility of a League of Nations, it has come into practical being under the pressure of events, and is already at work in advance of any formal constitution.

When this is generally understood (as it seems not yet to be) there is some danger that the necessity of equipping the League with a durable form and adequate organs may be overlooked.

The League stands for peace among nations assured by justice. But there can be no settled justice without judgment and no judgment without a tribunal.

It is true that the establishment of a regular Court of Nations demands full counsel and consideration, and cannot be hurried. This work may, and indeed must, wait for a time, and there is no harm in it if meanwhile the fundamental principles are observed.

Nevertheless the League will not be complete until it has

a proper judicial instrument as well as deliberative and executive bodies.

The essential rule for the prevention of war is that all members of the League are jointly and severally bound not to take the law into their own hands but to submit matters in dispute to some form of decision approved by the League. For the present this might be the existing tribunal of the Hague, or any special tribunal of arbitration agreed to by the parties under an existing treaty or otherwise.

But this will serve only for the present. The League has to rebuild and extend the law of nations, and a rule-making or even a legislative authority will not suffice for this. Formal definition and enactment must be kept alive by constructive interpretation, to the end of producing a continuous tradition of doctrine, a " jurisprudence " in the French sense of that word. Isolated decisions of different and independent authorities, however respectable, will never make such a doctrine.

Decision of actual disputes is not the only possible or desirable function of a Court of Nations. A Council which lays down or revises general rules should in every case have the best attainable information as to the existing rule or usage. It must know as accurately as may be whether there is any rule on the matter in hand, and in what respects amendment is called for. Such questions are unfit for discussion in a numerous deliberative assembly. Reference to a special expert commission in each case is possible, but reference to a standing body keeping a continuous record and tradition is far better. The most efficient body for this purpose would be a permanent judicial court (a); or, to put it conversely, a standing commission qualified to give the

(a) The British Empire affords an approximate precedent in the similar authority of the Judicial Committee of the Privy Council, quite lately exercised in the case of the Southern Rhodesian public lands.

Council expert and impartial advice would be no less qualified for the settlement of justiciable disputes.

The constitution of a court which would give due proportional weight to the Powers represented, together with adequate security for impartial judgment, is said to present formidable difficulties. Regarded as a problem in exact proportional representation, it is doubtless a hard matter. But a rough proportion good enough to be acceptable in practice is already attained in the various councils and committees of the Entente Powers at this moment working in Paris. In appointments to the Supreme Court of the United States it is understood that a certain balance shall be maintained among the groups of States which have distinct common interests. This is performed without any numerical rule, and indeed without any defined rule at all.

Further, it is said that a tribunal of nations cannot be impartial even when, according to the rule that no man should be judge in his own cause, members of the States immediately concerned are excluded. As to this it may be observed that there is no such man in the world as a judge who comes to the judgment seat with a wholly vacant mind. Extreme conscientiousness may even overshoot itself by carrying wilful reaction against a felt inclination too far the other way. But it is the common experience of the highest judicial tribunals in all civilised countries that the justice of the court is on the whole impartial. Exceptions may be noted in the history of international arbitration; but these were due to the mistake of appointing such arbitrators, and in such manner, that they were in effect rather advocates than judges. After all, a judicial habit of mind, and the community of ideas that springs from regular common action, are better safeguards than any mechanism of selection. Especially will this be so if the members of the court are not directly nominated by the constituent Governments of the League, which might be the more prudent way. At all events, many awards of a judicial nature and treaties pro-

moted by mediation or good offices of third parties have been
made in circumstances much less favourable to impartiality
than any reasonable frame of a standing international court
would be, and the sovereign Powers concerned have observed
them without question.

As in national, so in international law, the main object is
not to create an infallible tribunal (which is impossible)
but to provide for such administration of justice as will suffice
to maintain peace and order.

APPENDIX V.

———◆———

THE TWO BRANCHES OF THE MONROE DOCTRINE.

FROM PRESIDENT MONROE'S ADDRESS TO THE CONGRESS OF THE UNITED STATES, DEC. 1823.

A. . . . . The occasion [of discussions with the Russian Government as to commercial regulations in the Bering Straits, Alaska being then Russian territory] has been judged proper for asserting, as a principle in which the rights and interests of the United States are involved, that the American continents, by the free and independent condition which they have assumed and maintain, are henceforth not to be considered as subjects for future colonization by any European Powers.

———

Canning had nothing to do with this point, and, in common with other European statesmen, did not like Monroe's declaration. Inasmuch as there is now no unclaimed territory anywhere on the American continents, this branch of the Doctrine is obsolete.

Recent German ambition to establish German influence in a commanding position in South America would not have proceeded by any such crude method as open annexation. But the United States never undertook to acquiesce in every foreign enterprise that did not conflict with the Monroe Doctrine.

B. . . . . We owe it, therefore, to candor and to the amicable relations existing between the United States and those powers

[the Holy Alliance of Austria, Prussia, Russia, and France
under the restored Bourbon dynasty] to declare that we
should consider any attempt on their part to extend their
system to any portion of this hemisphere as dangerous to
our peace and safety. With the existing colonies or dependencies of any European power we have not interfered, and
shall not interfere. But with the governments who have
declared their independence and maintained it, and whose
independence we have, on great consideration and on just
principle, acknowledged, we could not view any interposition for the purpose of oppressing them, or controlling in
any other manner their destiny, by any European power in
any other light than as the manifestation of an unfriendly
disposition towards the United States. . . . It is impossible
that the allied powers should extend their political system
to any portion of either continent without endangering our
peace and happiness, nor can any one believe that our
Southern brethren, if left to themselves, would adopt it of
their own accord. It is equally impossible therefore that we
should behold such interposition, in any form, with indifference.

The precept "never to entangle ourselves in the broils of
Europe" is contained in a letter from Jefferson to Monroe,
and it is not included in the Monroe Doctrine, though it has
been commonly regarded as complementary to it. A plan
for preventing broils in Europe is certainly not within the
letter of Jefferson's warning.

A President's message to Congress has no binding authority of itself: the weight of the Monroe Doctrine is derived
from its adoption by successive American governments and
acceptance by public opinion. Monroe's actual words are a
historical document, not a statutory text.

APPENDIX VI.

—◆—

THE FOURTEEN POINTS.

[REPRINTED FOR REFERENCE FROM A LEAFLET ISSUED BY THE LEAGUE FOR PERMANENT PEACE OF BOSTON, MASS., NOV. 1918.]

What we seek is the reign of law, based upon the consent of the governed, and sustained by the organized opinion of mankind.—WOODROW WILSON, July 4, 1918.

PRESIDENT WILSON'S FOURTEEN POINTS.

THE BASIS OF THE NEW WORLD ORDER.

OPEN DEMOCRATIC DIPLOMACY.

1. Open covenants of peace, openly arrived at, after which there shall be no private international understandings of any kind but diplomacy shall proceed always frankly and in the public view.

FREEDOM OF THE SEAS (*a*).

2. Absolute freedom of navigation upon the seas, outside territorial waters, alike in peace and in war, except as the seas may be closed in whole or in part by international action for the enforcement of international covenants.

TOWARD THE REMOVAL OF ECONOMIC BARRIERS AND THE ESTABLISHMENT OF EQUAL TRADE CONDITIONS.

3. The removal, so far as possible, of all economic barriers and the establishment of an equality of trade conditions among all the nations consenting to the peace and associating themselves for its maintenance.

(*a*) With regard to the possible meanings of the term, a little book bearing it as title, by Mr. Charles Stewart Davison, New York, 1918, may be consulted with advantage.

REDUCTION OF ARMAMENTS UNDER GUARANTEES.

4. Adequate guarantees given and taken that national armaments will be reduced to the lowest points consistent with domestic safety.

NEW COLONIAL POLICIES BASED ON THE INTEREST OF THE
POPULATIONS CONCERNED.

5. A free, open-minded, and absolutely impartial adjustment of all colonial claims, based upon a strict observance of the principle that in determining all such questions of sovereignty the interests of the populations concerned must have equal weight with the equitable claims of the government whose title is to be determined.

RUSSIA.

6. The evacuation of all Russian territory and such a settlement of all questions affecting Russia as will secure the best and freest co-operation of the other nations of the world in obtaining for her an unhampered and unembarrassed opportunity for the independent determination of her own political development and national policy and assure her of a sincere welcome into the society of free nations under institutions of her own choosing; and more than a welcome, assistance also of every kind that she may need and may herself desire.

The treatment accorded Russia by her sister nations in the months to come will be the acid test of their good will, of their comprehension of her needs as distinguished from their own interests, and of their intelligent and unselfish sympathy.

RESTORATION OF BELGIUM.

7. Belgium, the whole world will agree, must be evacuated and restored, without any attempt to limit the sovereignty which she enjoys in common with all other free nations. No other single act will serve as this will serve to restore confidence among the nations in the laws which they have

themselves set and determined for the government of their relations with one another. Without this healing act the whole structure and validity of international law is forever impaired.

FRANCE AND ALSACE-LORRAINE.

8. All French territory should be freed and the invaded portions restored, and the wrong done to France by Prussia in 1871 in the matter of Alsace-Lorraine, which has unsettled the peace of the world for nearly fifty years, should be righted, in order that peace may once more be made secure in the interest of all.

"ITALIA IRREDENTA."

9. A readjustment of the frontiers of Italy should be effected along clearly recognizable lines of nationality.

AUSTRIA-HUNGARY.

10. The peoples of Austria-Hungary, whose place among the nations we wish to see safeguarded and assured, should be accorded the freest opportunity of autonomous development.

RESTORATION OF RUMANIA, SERBIA, AND MONTENEGRO; INTERNATIONAL GUARANTEES FOR THE BALKAN STATES.

11. Rumania, Serbia, and Montenegro should be evacuated; occupied territories restored; Serbia accorded free and secure access to the sea; and the relations of the several Balkan states to one another determined by friendly counsel along historically established lines of allegiance and nationality; and international guarantees of the political and economic independence and territorial integrity of the several Balkan states should be entered into.

TURKEY. DARDANELLES PERMANENTLY OPENED UNDER INTERNATIONAL GUARANTEES.

12. The Turkish portions of the present Ottoman Empire should be assured a secure sovereignty, but the other nation-

alities which are now under Turkish rule should be assured
an undoubted security of life and an absolutely unmolested
opportunity of autonomous development, and the Dardanelles
should be permanently opened as a free passage to the ships
and commerce of all nations, under international guarantees.

INDEPENDENCE OF POLAND.

13. An independent Polish state should be erected which
should include the territories inhabited by indisputably
Polish populations, which should be assured a free and
secure access to the sea, and whose political and economic
independence and territorial integrity should be guaranteed
by international covenant.

ESTABLISHMENT OF A LEAGUE OF NATIONS.

14. A general association of nations must be formed
under specific covenants for the purpose of affording mutual
guarantees of political independence and territorial integrity
to great and small states alike.

FROM PRESIDENT WILSON'S LIBERTY LOAN SPEECH, NEW YORK, SEPTEMBER 27, 1918.

"If it be in deed and truth the common object of the
governments associated against Germany and of the nations
whom they govern, as I believe it to be, to achieve by the
coming settlements a secure and lasting peace, it will be
necessary that all who sit down at the peace table shall
come ready and willing to pay the price, the only price,
that will procure it; and ready and willing, also, to create
in some virile fashion the only instrumentality by which it
can be made certain that the agreements of the peace will
be honored and fulfilled.

That price is impartial justice in every item of the settlement, no matter whose interest is crossed; and not only impartial justice, but also the satisfaction of the several peoples

whose fortunes are dealt with. That indispensable instrumentality is a League of Nations formed under covenants that will be efficacious. Without such an instrumentality, by which the peace of the world can be guaranteed, peace will rest in part upon the word of outlaws, and only upon that word. For Germany will have to redeem her character, not by what happens at the peace table but by what follows.

And, as I see it, the constitution of that League of Nations and the clear definition of its objects must be a part, is in a sense the most essential part, of the peace settlement itself. It cannot be formed now. If formed now, it would be merely a new alliance confined to the nations associated against a common enemy.

It is not likely that it could be formed after the settlement. It is necessary to guarantee the peace; and the peace cannot be guaranteed as an afterthought. The reason, to speak in plain terms again, why it must be guaranteed is that there will be parties to the peace whose promises have proved untrustworthy, and means must be found in connection with the peace settlement itself to remove that source of insecurity. It would be folly to leave the guarantee to the subsequent voluntary action of the Governments we have seen destroy Russia and deceive Roumania.

But these general terms do not disclose the whole matter. Some details are needed to make them sound less like a thesis and more like a practical program. These, then, are some of the particulars, and I state them with the greater confidence because I can state them authoritatively as representing this Government's interpretation of its own duty with regard to peace.

First, the impartial justice meted out must involve no discrimination between those to whom we wish to be just and those to whom we do not wish to be just. It must be a justice that plays no favorites and knows no standard but the equal rights of the several peoples concerned;

Second, no special or separate interest of any single nation or any group of nations can be made the basis of any part of the settlement which is not consistent with the common interest of all;

Third, there can be no leagues or alliances or special covenants and understandings within the general and common family of the League of Nations;

Fourth, and more specifically, there can be no special, selfish economic combinations within the league and no employment of any form of economic boycott or exclusion except as the power of economic penalty by exclusion from the markets of the world may be vested in the League of Nations itself as a means of discipline and control;

Fifth, all international agreements and treaties of every kind must be made known in their entirety to the rest of the world.

Special alliances and economic rivalries and hostilities have been the prolific source in the modern world of the plans and passions that produce war. It would be an insincere as well as an insecure peace that did not exclude them in definite and binding terms."

INDEX.

AGRICULTURE, INTERNATIONAL,
 Institute of, 82.

ALABAMA CASE, 32.

ALASKA
 boundary question, 3, 35.

ALLIED WESTERN POWERS
 agree to principle of League, 74.

ARBITRATION
 in Middle Ages, 3.
 modern revival of, 18.
 distinguished from mediation, 19.
 earlier than judicial decision, 23.
 criticisms on, 24, 27.
 rules guiding international, 28, 30.
 form of modern treaties, 36.
 procedure under Hague Conventions, 53.
 Tribunal, 54, *sqq.*
 summary procedure, 58.
 references of disputes under the Covenant, 135.

ARBITRATOR,
 authority of, 20.
 a temporary judge, 21.

ARMAMENT,
 national, not to be abolished, 152, 157.

ARMAMENTS,
    reduction of, 112.
    not dealt with at Hague Conferences, 113.

ARMS,
    private manufacture of, 115.
    prohibited kinds of, 117.

ASSEMBLY OF THE LEAGUE, 95.
    its constitution, 96, 98.
    voting power in, 99.
    competence of, 100.
    reference of disputes to, by request of parties or at
        discretion of Council, 143.

AWARD,
    arbitral, nature of, 19.
    compromise as possible element of, 31.

BALANCE OF POWER, 8.

BERLIN, CONGRESS OF, 13, 14.

BISMARCK, OTTO VON, 12.

BLOCKADE
    of State offending against the League, 147.
    pacific, now probably obsolete, 148.

BOURGEOIS, LÉON
    on amendments proposed by French Delegation, 125.

BRITISH EMPIRE,
    why no Secretariat? 109.

CHILE AND ARGENTINA,
    King Edward VII.'s award between, 36.

COMMISSIONS,
 international, to be under the League, 172.

COMMITTEES
 of the League, 107.

CONCERT OF EUROPE, 10, 14, 15.

CONCILIATION,
 powers of Council and Assembly to act as Boards of, 142.

CONFEDERATION, NORTH AMERICAN,
 Articles of, 101.

CONFERENCES AND CONGRESSES OF THE POWERS, 13.
 ——, Peace, 15.

CONSCRIPTION, 120.
 German form of, useless for war overseas, 122.

CONVENTIONS,
 of the Hague, 50.
 on international Commissions, 51.
 draft, as to permanent Court, 62.
 existing international, 80.

COUNCIL OF THE LEAGUE, 101.
 unanimity, 103.
 relation to the Assembly, 103.
 representation in, 104.
 to plan reduction of armaments, 114.
 advisory functions under Art. 10...128.
 to mediate in non-justiciable disputes, 142.
 may refer over to Assembly, 143.
 may work by committees, 144.
 duty of to recommend necessary action to protect
  covenants, 146.
 no compulsory authority, 149.

COURT,
> a transitory arbitral tribunal is not, 22.
> whether the Hague Tribunal is properly so called, 59.
> proposal of 1907 to establish a permanent, 61.
> renewal of proposal in 1914...64.
> the future permanent international, 139.

COVENANT,
> of the League, exposition of, 91, *sqq*.
> amendments to, 174.

DISARMAMENT
> not compulsory on members of the League, 112.

DOGGER BANK INCIDENT, 51.

DOMINIONS
> as members of League, 91.

DU BOIS, PIERRE,
> his project, 5.

EXPERIENCE,
> historical value of, 158.

FEDERATIONS AND FEDERAL ALLIANCES, 4.

GENEVA,
> seat of the League, 110.
> acceptance of the Canton, 111.

GREAT BRITAIN,
> reasons for her system of voluntary service, 121.

GREAT POWERS,
> concert of, 10, 14.

GROTIUS, HUGO, 8.

" Honour and Vital Interests,"
recent treaties for settling disputes without exception
of, 38.

Information,
military, exchange of, 119.

International Law
in early stages, 8.
its uncertainty exaggerated, 29.

Intervention
in domestic affairs, not warranted by Art. 10...127.

Ireland,
autonomy of, whether a question for the League, 131.

Kinglake, A. W.,
on usage of Europe, 9.
on effect of Crimean war, 11.

League of Nations,
societies for promoting, 70, 73, 83.
to assume direction of international commissions, 83.
formation of, 88.
not a super-State, 90, 94.
members of, 91.
recognition of in peace treaties, 92.
its organs, 95.
the Assembly, 98.
the Council, 101.
committee work in, 107.
the Secretariat, 108.
seat of, 110.
members guaranteed against external aggression, 127.

LEAGUE OF NATIONS—*continued*.
    membership may be forfeited by breach of covenant, 146.
    disputes between States not members of, 154.
    in relation to mandatory States, 169.
    to assume direction of international bureaux, 172.
    the spirit of its work, 176.

LEAGUE OF NATIONS UNION,
    formation of, 74.
    conference with allied societies, 74.

LEAGUE TO ENFORCE PEACE,
    the American, 70.

MAJORITY,
    vote by, when admissible in Assembly and Council, 105.
    mandates, 166.

MARBURG, THEODORE,
    founder of League to enforce Peace, 71, 79.

MORE, SIR THOMAS, 4.

MUNITIONS,
    private manufacture of, 115.

NAPOLEON, III., 11.

NICOLAS II. OF RUSSIA,
    convened first Peace Conference, 48.

PACIFISTS,
    perversity of, 73.

PARKER, LORD, OF WADDINGTON,
    his speech in the House of Lords, 75.

Peace,
  emergency powers of League as security for, 151.
  the King's, in English History, 155.

" Peace Commissions,"
  established by recent treaties, 39.

Peace Conferences
  of 1899...48.
  of 1907...49.

Penn, William,
  his essay, 5, 7.

Pessimists, 27, 29.

Poison,
  use of, in war, forbidden from ancient times, 118.

Police,
  cosmopolitan mixed force impracticable, 152.

Postal Union, 81.

Prussian General Staff,
  its War Book, 64.

Red Cross,
  work of, to be promoted by the League, 173.

Root, Elihu,
  his views of international sanctions, 67, 68.

Smuts, Gen. J. C.,
  his " practical suggestion," 77.
  on peace activities of the League, 168.

SOVEREIGNTY
    already limited by international conventions, 80.
    of members of League in domestic matters, 128.

STAFF, GENERAL,
    whether possible for the League, 123.
    can the League do without? 123, 149.

TAFT, WILLIAM H.,
    founder of League to enforce Peace, 70.

TREATIES,
    interpretation of, 31.

TRIBUNAL, ARBITRAL,
    modes of constituting, 34.

UNANIMITY,
    when required in Assembly and Council, 105.

UNITED STATES,
    army of, 122.

VIENNA, CONGRESS OF, 10.

WAR,
    supposed permanent necessity of, 25.
    to ensue *ipso facto* on breach of covenant, 76, 79.
    laws of, discredited and disregarded by Germans, 119
    threats or danger of, concern the whole League, 130.
    not to be resorted to till after award, &c., 134.
    restraint of, in case of non-member States, 154.
    contrary to covenants, act of war against the League,
        146.

WAR OF 1914,
unexpected outcome of, 87.

WASHINGTON, TREATY OF, 33.

WOMEN
eligible for all offices in the League, 110.

WOOLF, L. S.,
his reports to Fabian Society, 80.

PRINTED BY C. F. ROWORTH, 88, FETTER LANE, E.C. 4.

www.ingramcontent.com/pod-product-compliance
Lightning Source LLC
Chambersburg PA
CBHW031546260326
41914CB00002B/285